Intermediate English

Written by

Suzanne McQuade

Edited by

Laura Riggio

LIVING LANGUAGE®

Published in the United States by Living Language, an imprint of Random House, Inc.

www.livinglanguage.com

Editor: Laura Riggio
Production Editor: Ciara Robinson
Production Manager: Tom Marshall
Interior Design: Sophie Chin
Illustrations: Sophie Chin

First Edition

ISBN: 978-0-307-97234-7

This book is available at special discounts for bulk purchases for sales promotions or premiums. Special editions, including personalized covers, excerpts of existing books, and corporate imprints, can be created in large quantities for special needs. For more information, write to Special Markets/ Premium Sales, 1745 Broadway, MD 3-1, New York, New York 10019 or e-mail specialmarkets@ randomhouse.com.

PRINTED IN THE UNITED STATES OF AMERICA

10 9 8 7 6 5 4 3 2 1

Acknowledgments

Thanks to the Living Language team: Amanda D'Acierno, Christopher Warnasch, Suzanne McQuade, Laura Riggio, Erin Quirk, Heather Dalton, Amanda Munoz, Fabrizio LaRocca, Siobhan O'Hare, Sophie Chin, Pat Stango, Sue Daulton, Alison Skrabek, Ciara Robinson, Andrea McLin, and Tom Marshall.

COURSE

OUTLINE

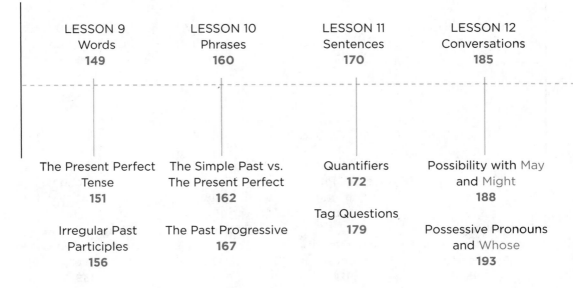
COURSE

O U T L I N E

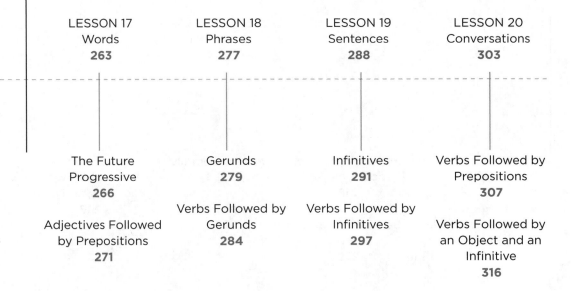

How to Use This Course

Welcome to *Living Language Intermediate English*! Before we begin, let's take a quick look at what you'll see in this course.

CONTENT

Intermediate English is a continuation of *Essential English*. It will review, expand on, and add to the foundation that you received in *Essential English*. In other words, this course contains an in-depth review of important vocabulary and grammar from *Essential English*; an expanded and more advanced look at some key vocabulary and grammar from *Essential English*; an introduction to idiomatic language and more challenging English grammar.

UNITS

There are five units in this course. Each unit has four lessons arranged in a "building block" structure: the first lesson will present essential *words*, the second will introduce longer *phrases*, the third will teach *sentences*, and the fourth will show how everything works together in everyday *conversations*.

At the beginning of each unit is an introduction highlighting what you'll learn in that unit. At the end of each unit you'll find the Unit Essentials, which reviews the key information from that unit, and a self-graded Unit Quiz, which tests what you've learned.

LESSONS

There are four lessons per unit for a total of 20 lessons in the course. Each lesson has the following components:

- **Introduction** outlining what you will cover in the lesson.

- **Word Builder 1** (first lesson of the unit) presenting key words and phrases.

- **Phrase Builder 1** (second lesson of the unit) introducing longer phrases and expressions.

- **Sentence Builder 1** (third lesson of the unit) teaching sentences.

- **Conversation 1** (fourth lesson of the unit) for a natural dialogue that brings together important vocabulary and grammar from the unit.

- **Word/Phrase/Sentence/Conversation Practice 1** practicing what you learned in Word Builder 1, Phrase Builder 1, Sentence Builder 1, or Conversation 1.

- **Grammar Builder 1** guiding you through important English grammar that you need to know.

- **Work Out 1** for a comprehensive practice of what you saw in Grammar Builder 1.

- **Word Builder 2/Phrase Builder 2/Sentence Builder 2/Conversation 2** for more key words, phrases, or sentences, or a second dialogue.

- **Word/Phrase/Sentence/Conversation Practice 2** practicing what you learned in Word Builder 2, Phrase Builder 2, Sentence Builder 2, or Conversation 2.

- **Grammar Builder 2** for more information on English grammar.

- **Work Out 2** for a comprehensive practice of what you saw in Grammar Builder 2.

- **Drive It Home** ingraining an important point of English grammar for the long term.

- **Tip** or **Culture Note** for a helpful language tip or useful cultural information related to the lesson or unit.

- **How Did You Do?** outlining what you learned in the lesson.

- **Word Recall** reviewing important vocabulary and grammar from the lesson.

- **Take It Further** sections appear throughout the lessons, providing extra information about new vocabulary, expanding on certain grammar points, or introducing additional words and phrases.

UNIT QUIZ

After each Unit, you'll see a **Unit Quiz.** The quizzes are self-graded so it's easy for you to test your progress and see if you should go back and review.

PROGRESS BAR

You will see a **Progress Bar** on each page that has course material. It indicates your current position within the unit and lets you know how much progress you're making. Each line in the bar represents a Grammar Builder section.

AUDIO

Look for the symbol ⊙ to help guide you through the audio as you're reading the book. It will tell you which track to listen to for each section that has audio. When you see the symbol, select the indicated track and start listening. If you don't see the symbol, then there isn't any audio for that section.

You can listen to the audio on its own, when you're on the go, to brush up on your pronunciation or review what you've learned in the book.

GRAMMAR SUMMARY

At the back of this book you will find a **Grammar Summary**. The Grammar Summary is a reference for grammar points such as irregular verb forms, prepositions following adjectives and verbs, verbs followed by gerunds, and verbs and adjectives followed by infinitives.

FREE ONLINE TOOLS

Go to **www.livinglanguage.com/languagelab** to access your free online tools. The tools are organized around the units in this course, with audiovisual flashcards, and interactive games and quizzes. These tools will help you to review and practice the vocabulary and grammar that you've seen in the units, as well as provide some bonus words and phrases related to the unit's topic.

Unit 1:
The Daily Routine

Welcome to Unit 1. This unit is about your daily routine. We'll review important basic vocabulary for your **house** and your **day**. We'll also review the simple present (**goes**) and the present progressive (**is going**). You'll also learn how to give commands (**go home!**), and how to use object pronouns like **me** and **to me**. Unit 1 covers common prepositions (**in**, **at**, **to**, **toward**) and useful pronouns like **someone** and **something**. Finally, you'll learn much more about the articles **the** and **a/an**, and we'll look at **some** and **any** again.

Lesson 1: Words

In this lesson you'll learn:

☐ the names of everyday objects and other essential vocabulary

☐ how to use the simple present (**goes**) and the present progressive (**is going**)

☐ the most common verbs and other essential vocabulary

☐ how to give commands

The Simple Present and the
Present Progressive

Object Pronouns

Commands and
Requests

Indirect Objects

Word Builder 1

▶ 1A Word Builder 1 (CD 4, Track 2)

Here is some key vocabulary that you should know for Unit 1. Let's look at the **rooms** in a **house**, as well as some common items you'll find in them.

rooms: living room, dining room, kitchen, bedroom, bathroom, study	
parts of a house: roof, wall, floor, ceiling, door, window, basement, attic, closet, hall	
appliances: refrigerator, stove, oven, microwave, dishwasher, toaster, coffee maker, washing machine, dryer	
furniture: couch, chair, table, desk, bed, dresser	
kitchen: cabinets, drawers, cupboard	
bathroom: toilet, shower, bath, towel, sink, medicine cabinet	

✎ Word Practice 1

Let's review basic vocabulary.

1. Which room is the refrigerator in?

   _____

2. Which room is the couch and the television in?

   _____

3. Which rooms have sinks?

_____

4. What furniture is in the bedroom?

_____

5. What are the names of some appliances?

_____

6. A room usually has four ...

_____

7. Which room usually has a big table and chairs?

_____

8. What do you find in a bathroom?

_____

ANSWER KEY
1. the kitchen; 2. the living room; 3. the kitchen and the bathroom; 4. a bed, a dresser, maybe a desk and a chair, a small table or two; 5. a refrigerator, a stove, an oven, a microwave, a dishwasher, a toaster, a coffee maker, a washing machine, a dryer; 6. walls; 7. the dining room; 8. the toilet, the shower, the bath, some towels, a sink, a medicine cabinet

Take It Further
BE **AND** HAVE

In *Essential English,* you learned the verbs **be** and **have**. Let's review.

I am/I'm	we are/we're
you are/you're	you are/you're
he is, she is, it is/he's, she's, it's	they are/they're

The Simple Present and the
Present Progressive

Object Pronouns

Commands and
Requests

Indirect Objects

I have/I've	we have/we've
you have/we've	you have/you've
he has, she has, it has/ he's, she's, it's	they have/they've

Remember that the negative of **be** only uses **not**. For **I**, there are two negative forms, but for **you**, **he**, **she**, **it**, **we**, and **they**, there are three.

I am not/I'm not	we are not/we're not/we aren't
you are not/you're not/you aren't	you are not/you're not/you aren't
he is not, she is not, it is not/ he's not, she's not, it's not/ he isn't, she isn't, it isn't	they are not/they're not/they aren't

The negative of **have** uses **do** (with **I**, **you**, **we**, and **they**) or **does** (with **he**, **she**, and **it**). After **does not** or **doesn't**, **has** becomes **have**: he <u>has</u>, but he does not <u>have</u>.

I do not have/I don't have	we do not have/we don't have
you do not have/you don't have	you do not have/you don't have
he/she/it does not have he/she/it doesn't have	they do not have/they don't have

To form a question with **be**, put the verb first.

Am I?	Are we?
Are you?	Are you?
Is he/she/it?	Are they?

But to form a question with **have** or any other verb, put **do** or **does** first.

Do I have?	Do we have?
Do you have?	Do you have?
Does he/she/it have?	Do they have?

Grammar Builder 1

▶ 1B Grammar Builder 1 (CD 4, Track 3)

THE SIMPLE PRESENT AND THE PRESENT PROGRESSIVE

You learned the simple present tense in Lesson 5 of Essential English. For most verbs, just add **s** to the **he/she/it** form.

I work, see, speak	**we work, see, speak**
you work, see, speak	**you work, see, speak**
he/she/it works, sees, speaks	**they work, see, speak**

Verbs that end in **–ch, –sh, –s, –x,** and **–z** add **–es** instead of **–s** in the **he/she/it** form. Verbs that end in **–o** add **–es**, too, but it sounds like **–z**. Verbs that end in **–y** take **–ies** in the **he/she/it** form.

I watch, brush, fix, go, study	**we watch, brush, fix, go, study**
you watch, brush, fix, go, study	**you watch, brush, fix, go, study**
he/she/it watches, brushes, fixes, goes, studies	**they watch, brush, fix, go, study**

Form questions and negatives in the simple present with **do** or **does**. Remember that the **–(e)s** of the **he/she/it** form is not used on the main verb with **does**: he goes, he doesn't go, does he go?

They work in the city. **They don't work in the city.** **Do they work in the city?**	
The boy brushes his teeth after dinner. **The boy doesn't brush his teeth after dinner.** **Does the boy brush his teeth after dinner?**	

The Simple Present and the
Present Progressive

Object Pronouns

Commands and
Requests

Indirect Objects

You speak Cantonese at home.	
Do you speak Cantonese at home?	
You don't speak Cantonese at home.	

You learned the present progressive in Lesson 9 of *Essential English*. It uses a form of be with the –ing form of the main verb.

I am working, speaking, reading	we are working, speaking, reading
you are working, speaking, reading	you are working, speaking, reading
he/she/it is working, speaking, reading	they are working, speaking, reading

Verbs that end in a silent –e (take, write, wake) drop the –e before –ing: taking, writing, waking. And one-syllable verbs that end in a single consonant (put, swim, stop) double the consonant before –ing: putting, swimming, stopping. But do not double final –x or –w: fix, fixing; grow, growing. Do not change –y before –ing: study, studying; dry, drying.

Be comes before the –ing form of the main verb in questions. In the negative, put not between be and the –ing form of the main verb.

She is working this weekend.	
Is she working this weekend?	
She is not working this weekend.	
They are taking the train to work.	
Are they taking the train to work?	
They are not taking the train to work.	
The girl is swimming in the lake.	
The girl is not swimming in the lake.	
Is the girl swimming in the lake?	

The simple present is used to make general statements, or to express habits. It is used with expressions like **always**, **never**, **generally**, **usually**, **on Tuesdays**, **every day**, **every week**, and so on.

I always take the bus to work.	
They never go to school on Sundays.	
Sarah watches television and then reads every night.	
People in France eat a lot of cheese.	

The present progressive is used to express something that is happening **now**.

You are studying English right now.	
It's Tuesday morning, so John is working.	
Julio is with his family now, so he's speaking Spanish.	
It's only four thirty in the afternoon, so they're not eating dinner now.	

The present progressive is also used to express the future.

What are you doing tomorrow night?	
Next week we're going to a new restaurant.	
We're leaving for the airport in an hour.	
I'm going home tonight after work.	

There are certain verbs—called stative verbs—that you should avoid using in the present progressive tense for now: **be**, **forget**, **have**, **know**, **like**, **love**, **mean**, **see**, and **smell**. You will eventually see these verbs used in the progressive, such as

The Simple Present and the
Present Progressive

Object Pronouns

Commands and
Requests

Indirect Objects

I'm having a party, or **I'm smelling a rose**, but don't worry about that for now. You will learn more about how and when to use these verbs in the progressive in *Advanced English*. Until then, when you want to use these verbs in the present, use the simple present tense.

Take It Further

HOW TO PRONOUNCE THE ENDINGS –S AND –ES

Plural nouns and the he/she/it form of verbs take the endings –s and –es in English. The pronunciation rules are the same. If the noun or verb ends in a p, k, t, or f sound pronounce –s like /s/ in **kiss** or **miss**.

HE/SHE/IT VERBS	PLURAL NOUNS
stops, wraps	cups, tops
talks, takes	cakes, bikes
writes, fights	aunts, cats
whiffs, sniffs	roofs, puffs

Remember that the rule is about the sounds, not necessarily the spelling. **Write** and **cake** end in –e in spelling, but in t and k in pronunciation, so the ending –s is pronounced /s/.

If a word ends in a ch, sh, s, x, j, or z sound, the ending is spelled –es, which is always pronounced /iz/, rhyming with **his**. Remember that the spelling –ge is often pronounced /j/, and –se is often pronounced /z/.

HE/SHE/IT VERBS	PLURAL NOUNS
watches, touches	inches, couches
brushes, pushes	wishes, bushes
kisses, misses	races, prices
fixes, relaxes	faxes, boxes
pledges, ages	barges, messages
dazes, organizes	sizes, mazes

If a word ends in any other consonant sound (but see the note on –th), or a vowel sound, the ending –s is pronounced /z/.

HE/SHE/IT VERBS	PLURAL NOUNS
grabs	tubs
gags	bags
comes	drums
wins	cans
sings	wings
pulls	halls
tears	pears
lives	wives
says, plays, blows, does, sees	photos, days, seas, boys, brews

Remember that the spelling th has two different pronunciations. One is called "voiced," because you can feel vibration in your throat when you say it: bathe, soothe, writhe, teethe. (Don't worry if you don't know these verbs! Most are not common.) The other pronunciation is "voiceless," because there is no vibration:

The Simple Present and the
Present Progressive

Object Pronouns

Commands and
Requests

Indirect Objects

bath, width, wreath, froth. After voiced th, the ending –s is pronounced as /z/, and after voiceless th, the ending –s is pronounced /s/.

VOICED TH	VOICELESS TH
bathes	baths
soothes	widths
writhes	froths
teethes	wreaths

✎ Work Out 1

Choose the most logical verb, and write the correct form, in either the simple present or the present progressive.

1. Bob_____ in an office every weekday. (sleep, sing, work)

2. This weekend I_____ my parents in the country.

   (talk, visit, go)

3. Harold_____ Italian, French, and English. (speak, have, get)

4. It's 7:00, so they_____ dinner now. (drink, study, eat)

5. There_____ three bedrooms in the house. (have, be, make)

6. We_____ the train to the city tomorrow morning.

   (go, take, drive)

7. John_____ Chinese at the university next year.

   (know, write, study)

8. The kids_____ in the lake every weekend. (**swim, eat, read**)

9. Marsha_____ every night before bed. (**drive, be, read**)

10. Does Bob_____ wine with dinner every night? (**eat, drink, make**)

ANSWER KEY
1. works; 2. am visiting; 3. speaks; 4. are eating; 5. are; 6. are taking; 7. is studying; 8. swim;
9. reads; 10. drink

Word Builder 2

▶ 1C Word Builder 2 (CD 4, Track 4)

Here is some more important vocabulary for Unit 1. Do you know these common verbs?

be (am, is, are), have (has)	
make, do, get	
speak, say, tell, ask, answer	
see, hear, listen to, smell, taste, touch	
cook, eat, drink	
go, come, walk, run, drive	
take, give, send, bring	
play, run, jump, swim	
like, love, enjoy, dislike, hate	
arrive, visit, stay, leave	
open, close	
wake up, brush your teeth, wash, take a shower, shave, get dressed, work, eat, go to bed, sleep	
study, read, write, think, remember, forget, know	

✎ Word Practice 2

Choose the best verb.

1. I_____ every morning at seven thirty.

   a. brush

   b. wake up

   c. know

   d. like

2. The children are_____ a game.

   a. swimming

   b. running

   c. jumping

   d. playing

3. Our friends from France_____ every year.

   a. visit

   b. see

   c. eat

   d. take

4. Bill_____ to music while he studies.

   a. hears

   b. listens

   c. reads

   d. writes

5. We're_____ the house at seven and getting to the airport at nine.

  a. **getting**

  b. **taking**

  c. **leaving**

  d. **going**

6. Ron_____ seven hours every night.

  a. **eats**

  b. **goes to bed**

  c. **gets up**

  d. **sleeps**

7. We go to the beach and_____ in the ocean every Saturday.

  a. **write**

  b. **swim**

  c. **take**

  d. **study**

8. What are you_____, a book or a magazine?

  a. **studying**

  b. **listening to**

  c. **reading**

  d. **eating**

9. We're_____ at a really nice hotel in Paris.

  a. **staying**

The Simple Present and the
Present Progressive

Object Pronouns

Commands and
Requests

Indirect Objects

b. **going**

c. **coming**

d. **leaving**

10. I don't_____ his name.

   a. **answer**

   b. **say**

   c. **take**

   d. **know**

ANSWER KEY
1. b; 2. d; 3. a; 4. b; 5. c; 6. d; 7. b; 8. c; 9. a; 10. d

Grammar Builder 2

▶ 1D Grammar Builder 2 (CD 4, Track 5)

COMMANDS AND REQUESTS

Use the simple form of the verb, without –s, to give a command. Add **please** to be polite.

Go outside and play, kids!	
Listen to the question and give the correct answer.	
Please say hello to your wife for me.	
Please bring me a glass of water.	

Use **do not** or **don't** in negative commands.

It's a beautiful day, don't stay in the house!	

Don't watch television during dinner.	
Please don't talk in the library.	
Please don't be late.	

Very polite commands or requests use **could you (please)** or **would you (please)**.

Would you please pass me the salt?	
Could you please come to the office early tomorrow?	

The negative uses **would you (please) not** or **could you (please) not**.

Would you please not talk so loudly?	
Could you please not listen to the radio during dinner?	

The expression **would you mind** and the **–ing** form of a verb is another way of expressing a polite command or request. In the negative, put **not** before the **–ing** verb.

Would you mind working late tonight?	
Would you mind driving me to the airport?	
Would you mind not eating in my office?	

Work Out 2

Make polite requests from the following commands. First use
Would you please … and then use **Would you mind …** Follow the example.

Commands and
Requests

Example: Open the door.

Answer: **Would you please open the door? Would you mind opening the door?**

1. Answer the question.

_____

2. Take this book.

_____

3. Send an e-mail.

_____

4. Drive the kids to school.

_____

5. Pass the salt.

_____

6. Don't speak in the classroom.

_____

7. Don't sit in front of the television.

_____

8. Don't call so early in the morning.

_____

ANSWER KEY

1. Would you please answer the question? Would you mind answering the question? 2. Would you please take this book? Would you mind taking this book? 3. Would you please send an e-mail? Would you mind sending an e-mail? 4. Would you please drive the kids to school? Would you mind driving the kids to school? 5. Would you please pass the salt? Would you mind passing the salt? 6. Would you please not speak in the classroom? Would you mind not speaking in the classroom? 7. Would you please not sit in front of the television? Would you mind not sitting in front of the

television? 8. Would you please not call so early in the morning? Would you mind not calling so early in the morning?

✎ Drive It Home

We will give you a verb; you conjugate it in the 3rd person (he/she/it) tense: first in the simple present tense, then in the present progressive.

1. take _____

2. love _____

3. put _____

4. stop _____

5. study _____

6. dry _____

7. see _____

8. go _____

9. wash _____

10. fix _____

ANSWER KEY
1. takes, is taking 2. loves, is loving 3. puts, is putting 4. stops, is stopping 5. studies, is studying
6. dries, is drying 7. sees, is seeing 8. goes, is going 9. washes, is washing 10. fixes, is fixing

How Did You Do?

Let's see how you did in this lesson. By now, you should know:

☐ the names of everyday objects and other essential vocabulary
(Still unsure? Jump back to page 14.)

☐ how to use the simple present (**goes**) and the present progressive (**is going**) (Still unsure? Jump back to page 17.)

☐ the most common verbs and other essential vocabulary (Still unsure? Jump back to page 23.)

☐ how to give commands (Still unsure? Jump back to page 26.)

✎ Word Recall

Which sound: /s/ or /z/? For each word below, state whether the **s** endings sound like an **s** or a **z** sound.

1. doors _____

2. tables _____

3. attics _____

4. beds _____

5. kitchens _____

6. toasters _____

7. watches _____

8. cooks _____

9. says _____

10. breathes _____

11. works _____

12. lives _____

ANSWER KEY
1. /z/; 2. /z/; 3. /s/; 4. /z/; 5. /z/; 6. /z/; 7. /z/; 8. /s/; 9. /z/; 10. /z/; 11. /s/; 12. /z/

Lesson 2: Phrases

In this lesson you'll learn:

☐ object pronouns (**me, him, her**)

☐ indirect objects (**to Sarah, to him, to the kids**)

Phrase Builder 1

▶ 2A Phrase Builder 1 (CD 4, Track 6)

Let's look at some expressions with get.

to get up	
to get undressed	
to get in the shower	
to get dressed	
to get coffee at the store	
to get on the train/bus	
to get to work at nine o'clock	
to get off the train/bus	
to get home at six in the evening	
to get hot	
to get cold	
to get tired	
to get hungry	
to get bored	
to get a new computer/car/job	
to get going	

✎ Phrase Practice 1

Fill in the blank with the missing word.

1. In winter, I get_____.

2. I get_____ at seven in the morning.

3. I get_____ before I take a shower.

4. When Sheila doesn't eat, she gets_____.

5. In summer, we get_____.

6. After his shower, Jim gets_____.

7. Rich leaves his apartment, walks to the train station, and gets_____ the train.

8. They get_____ work before nine o'clock every morning.

9. When the bus stops, I get_____ the bus and walk home.

10. It's late. Let's get_____.

ANSWER KEY
1. **cold**; 2. **up**; 3. **undressed**; 4. **hungry** 5. **hot**. 6. **dressed**; 7. **on**; 8. **to**; 9. **off**; 10. **going**

Grammar Builder 1

▶ 2B Grammar Builder 1 (CD 4, Track 7)

OBJECT PRONOUNS

You learned the subject pronouns in Lesson 1 of *Essential English*. There are also object pronouns. Use object pronouns after verbs and prepositions.

SUBJECT PRONOUNS	OBJECT PRONOUNS
I	me
you	you
he	him

SUBJECT PRONOUNS	OBJECT PRONOUNS
she	her
it	it
we	us
they	them

Remember that subject pronouns are used as the subject of a sentence:

John speaks French.
He speaks French.

Object pronouns are used as the direct object of a verb:

I see **John**.
I see **him**.

They're also used after prepositions, like with or next to.

We're having dinner with our friends.
We're having dinner with them.

Here are some more examples of subject and object pronouns.

She doesn't like me, and I don't like her.	
The kids? I see them. They're swimming in the lake.	
I know her. I sit next to her in Spanish class.	
Would you please come to the restaurant with us?	

✎ Work Out 1

Change the underlined noun to a subject or object pronoun. Follow the example.

Example: I see Mary.
Answer: **I see her.**

1. I hear Mr. Blake.

   _____

2. The kids are swimming in the lake.

   _____

3. Do you want to swim with the kids?

   _____

4. Joe likes Sarah very much.

   _____

5. Our friends visit my family and me every summer.

   _____

6. I work with Rebecca in a store downtown.

   _____

7. Do you know Pete Simmons?

   _____

8. Could you please bring your computer tomorrow?

   _____

9. John and Terry take the train to work.

   _____

10. Rob is coming to the restaurant with you and me tonight.

ANSWER KEY

1. I hear him. 2. They are swimming in the lake. 3. Do you want to swim with them? 4. Joe likes her very much. 5. Our friends visit us every summer. 6. I work with her in a store downtown. 7. Do you know him? 8. Could you please bring it tomorrow? 9. They take the train to work. 10. Rob is coming to the restaurant with us tonight.

Phrase Builder 2

▶ 2C Phrase Builder 2 (CD 4, Track 8)

Now let's look at some common expressions with take.

to take a shower	
to take a bath	
to take fifteen minutes on foot	
to take two hours by car	
to take a bus/train/plane	
to take a break	
to take medicine/aspirin	
to take a picture	
to take place	
to take a test	
Take care!	
Take it easy!	

✎ Phrase Practice 2

Fill in the blanks with the word that best completes the sentence.

1. My son is too young for a shower, so he's taking a_____.

2. You can walk to the restaurant from here. It only_____ ten minutes.

3. I'm tired. Can we take a_____?

4. Jane hates baths, so she's taking a_____.

5. You have to take a_____ from New York to Tokyo.

6. Do you have a headache? Take some_____.

7. The students are taking a_____ tomorrow, so they're studying now.

8. Can you take a_____ of us in front of the Eiffel Tower?

9. The drive from New York to Boston_____ about four and a half hours.

10. See you later! Take it_____!

ANSWER KEY
1. bath; 2. takes; 3. break; 4. shower; 5. plane; 6. aspirin; 7. test; 8. picture; 9. takes; 10. easy

Grammar Builder 2
▶ 2D Grammar Builder 2 (CD 4, Track 9)

INDIRECT OBJECTS

Verbs like give, bring, send, write, show, get, and buy take <u>direct objects</u>:

She gives <u>a lot of presents</u> at Christmas.	
Bring <u>wine</u> for the dinner party.	
I'm sending <u>an e-mail</u> from my phone.	
We're writing <u>a letter</u>.	
I'm showing <u>my apartment</u>.	
Jill is getting <u>a computer</u>.	
I'm buying <u>groceries</u>.	

These verbs can also take <u>indirect objects</u>, along with direct objects. The indirect object can be a noun, and it comes after the direct object and the preposition to or for. To is used with most verbs, but for is used with get, buy, and some others.

She gives a lot of presents <u>to her friends</u> at Christmas.	
Bring wine <u>to Sue and Bob</u> for the dinner party.	
I'm sending an e-mail <u>to my boss</u> from my phone.	
We're writing a letter <u>to our parents</u>.	
I'm showing my apartment <u>to my friends</u>.	
Jill is getting a computer <u>for her husband</u>.	
I'm buying groceries <u>for my mother</u>.	

The indirect object can also be a pronoun. Use the same object pronouns that you learned in Grammar Builder 1 after the preposition to or for.

She gives a lot of presents <u>to them</u> at Christmas.	
Bring wine <u>to them</u> for the dinner party.	
I'm sending an e-mail <u>to her</u> from my phone.	
We're writing a letter <u>to them</u>.	
I'm showing my apartment <u>to them</u>.	
Jill is getting a computer <u>for him</u>.	
I'm buying groceries <u>for her</u>.	

The Simple Present and the
Present Progressive

Object Pronouns

Commands and
Requests

Indirect Objects

✎ Work Out 2

Rewrite the sentences with indirect object nouns and pronouns, following the example.

Example: We're giving a present. (Jack)
Answer: **We're giving a present to Jack. We're giving a present to him.**

1. The waiter is giving the menu. (the customers)

   _____

2. We're bringing a cake. (our grandmother)

   _____

3. The boys send messages from their phones. (their friends)

   _____

4. Kate is writing a letter. (John)

   _____

5. Joe is buying flowers. (his girlfriend)

   _____

ANSWER KEY
1. The waiter is giving the menu to the customers. The waiter is giving the menu to them. 2. We're bringing a cake to our grandmother. We're bringing a cake to her. 3. The boys send messages to their friends from their phones. The boys send messages to them from their phones. 4. Kate is writing a letter to John. Kate is writing a letter to him. 5. Joe is buying flowers for his girlfriend. Joe is buying flowers for her.

✎ Drive It Home

Change the underlined word to the appropriate object pronoun.

1. Bring the flowers to <u>Mary</u>.

_____

2. Take the cake to <u>your grandmother</u>.

_____

3. Tell <u>your mother</u> what you heard.

_____

4. We're having dinner with <u>Angela</u> tonight.

_____

Joe likes <u>Sarah</u> very much.

_____

Visit <u>the Blake family</u> when you're in town.

_____

5. He is eating with <u>Angela and Sarah</u> after work.

_____

6. Bring the flowers to <u>your grandmother and grandfather</u>.

_____

7. Bring <u>the flowers</u> to your grandmother and grandfather.

_____

8. Give <u>the kids</u> some chocolate.

_____

ANSWER KEY
1-5 all **her**; 6-10 all **them**

The Simple Present and the
Present Progressive

Object Pronouns

Commands and
Requests

Indirect Objects

How Did You Do?

Let's see how you did in this lesson. By now, you should know:

☐ object pronouns (me, him, her) (Still unsure? Jump back to page 32.)

☐ indirect objects (to Sarah, to him, to the kids)
(Still unsure? Jump back to page 36.)

✎ Word Recall

Let's review expressions with get and take. Circle the word that goes best with each expression.

1. to (get/take) a bath

2. to (get/take) going

3. to (get/take) hot

4. to (get/take) a break

5. to (get/take) a test

6. to (get/take) tired

7. (Get/Take) care!

8. to (get/take) off the train

9. to (get/take) fifteen minutes on foot

10. to (get/take) hungry

11. to (get/take) up

12. to (get/take) place

ANSWER KEY

1. to take a bath; 2. to get going; 3. to get hot; 4. to take a break; 5. to take a test; 6. to get tired; 7. Take care! 8. to get off the train; 9. to take fifteen minutes on foot; 10. to get hungry; 11. to get up; 12. to take place

Lesson 3: Sentences

In this lesson you'll learn:

☐ how to use the double object construction (**give Mary/her a book**)

☐ the most common prepositions of location (**at, in**) and direction (**to, toward**)

☐ the difference between **say** and **tell**

Sentence Builder 1

▶ 3A Sentence Builder 1 (CD 4, Track 10)

There are seven rooms in our house.	
The living room is big and comfortable.	
There's a couch, two chairs, a coffee table, and a television in the living room.	
The dining room is small, but we have a table and four chairs in it.	
The kitchen is sunny, but old, so we're renovating it.	
We're getting new appliances—a new refrigerator, a new stove, a new oven, and a new dishwasher.	

The Simple Present and the
Present Progressive

Object Pronouns

Commands and
Requests

Indirect Objects

I hate the old cabinets, but the new ones are very nice.	
The cabinets are full of dishes and food.	
They're very disorganized; they're a mess!	
The bedrooms are small, but they have big closets.	
We're also renovating the bathroom.	
We're getting new tiles for the floor, and a new toilet and shower.	

✎ Sentence Practice 1

Listen to your audio again, and fill in the missing words that you hear.

1. There are seven_____ in our house.

2. The_____room is big and _____.

3. There's a_____, two _____, a coffee _____, and a television in the living room.

4. The_____ room is small, but we have a table and four chairs in _____.

5. The_____ is sunny, but old, so we're _____ it.

6. We're getting new_____—a new refrigerator, a new stove, a new oven, and a new _____.

7. I_____ the old _____, but the new ones are very nice.

8. The cabinets are_____ of dishes and food.

9. They're very disorganized; they're a_____!

10. The_____ are small, but they have big _____.

11. We're_____ renovating the bathroom.

12. We're getting new_____ for the floor, and a new toilet and

_____.

ANSWER KEY

1. rooms; 2. living, comfortable; 3. couch, chairs, table; 4. dining, it; 5. kitchen, renovating;
6. appliances, dishwasher; 7. hate, cabinets; 8. full; 9. mess; 10. bedrooms, closets; 11. also;
12. tiles, shower

Grammar Builder 1

▶ 3B Grammar Builder 1 (CD 4, Track 11)

DOUBLE OBJECTS

In the last lesson, you learned about indirect object nouns and pronouns that use
the prepositions **to** or **for**.

She gives a lot of presents <u>to her friends</u> at Christmas.	
I'm sending an e-mail <u>to my boss</u> from my phone.	

You can also put indirect object nouns and pronouns between the verb and the
direct object. In this case, do not use the preposition **to** or **for**.

She gives <u>her friends</u> a lot of presents at Christmas. She gives <u>them</u> a lot of presents.	

The Simple Present and the
Present Progressive

Object Pronouns

Commands and
Requests

Indirect Objects

Bring <u>Sue and Bob</u> wine for the dinner party. **Bring <u>them</u> wine for the dinner party.**	
I'm sending <u>my boss</u> an e-mail from my phone. **I'm sending <u>him</u> an e-mail from my phone.**	
We're writing <u>our parents</u> a letter. **We're writing <u>them</u> a letter.**	
I'm showing <u>my friends</u> my apartment. **I'm showing <u>them</u> my apartment.**	
Jill is getting <u>her husband</u> a computer. **Jill is getting <u>him</u> a computer.**	
I'm buying <u>my mother</u> groceries. **I'm buying <u>her</u> groceries.**	

If both the direct object and the indirect object are pronouns, the order is:
verb + direct object pronoun + to/for + indirect object pronoun

She gives them to me.	
Bring it to them.	
I'm sending it to him.	
We're writing it to you.	
He's showing them to me.	
Gary's getting it for us.	
I'm buying them for her.	

Double Objects

Indefinite and Other Pronouns

Prepositions of Location
and Direction

Definite Articles, Indefinite
Articles, and "Bare" Nouns

Take It Further
SAY AND TELL

The common verbs say and tell are similar in meaning, but not identical. Use say when you want to talk about speaking in general, for example when you repeat someone's words. Say often does not have an indirect object. But when it does, it always uses to.

John says good morning every day. John says good morning to me every day.	
Our teacher always says, "Do your homework tonight, class!" Our teacher always says to us, "Do your homework tonight, class!"	

Use tell when you want to talk about something specific, for example an answer, a name, a telephone number, or other specific information. Tell always has an indirect object, usually without to.

The students tell the teacher their names. The students tell her their names.	
Our kids always tell their parents their weekend plans. Our kids always tell us their weekend plans.	

Compare say and tell in questions. Say uses to, but tell does not.

What do the students say to their teacher?	

The Simple Present and the
Present Progressive
Object Pronouns

Commands and
Requests
Indirect Objects

What do the students tell their teacher?	

✎ Work Out 1

Answer the questions, following the example. Use an indirect object pronoun, and a direct object noun.

Example: What is John getting for Bill? (a book)
Answer: He's getting him a book.

1. What are you cooking for your girlfriend? (pasta)

   _____

2. What is Paul sending to his grandparents? (a postcard)

   _____

3. What is the waiter giving to Steve? (the wine list)

   _____

4. What are your friends bringing to you and me? (a computer)

   _____

5. What is Sue buying for her husband? (a new shirt)

   _____

6. What are the kids writing to their parents? (letters)

   _____

7. What is the professor giving to her students? (their tests)

8. What is the salesman showing to Jack? (an expensive car)

ANSWER KEY
1. I'm cooking her pasta. 2. He's sending them a postcard. 3. He's giving him the wine list. 4. They're bringing us a computer. 5. She's buying him a new shirt. 6. They're writing them letters. 7. She's giving them their tests. 8. He's showing him an expensive car.

Sentence Builder 2

▶ 3C Sentence Builder 2 (CD 4, Track 12)

What are you doing this weekend? Do you have any plans?	
We're visiting friends in the city.	
We're going out to dinner and then to a play.	
Bill is visiting his parents in the country.	
They have a house on a lake in the mountains.	
How long does it take to drive there?	
It takes two and a half hours by car.	
What does he do at his parents' lake house?	
Bill swims or walks in the woods during the day.	
In the evening he eats with his parents, and then reads or watches television.	

The Simple Present and the
Present Progressive

Object Pronouns

Commands and
Requests

Indirect Objects

He spends a lot of time in the country, but he loves the city, too.	

✎ Sentence Practice 2

Listen to your audio again, and fill in the missing words that you hear.

1. What are you doing this weekend? Do you have any_____?

2. We're_____ friends in the city.

3. We're_____ to dinner and then to a play.

4. Bill is visiting his parents in the_____.

5. They have a house_____ a lake _____ the mountains.

6. How_____ does it _____to drive there?

7. It takes two and a_____ hours by _____.

8. What_____ he _____ at his parents' lake house?

9. Bill swims or walks_____ the woods _____ the day.

10. In the evening he_____ with his parents, and then _____ or _____ television.

11. He_____ a lot of time in the country, but he loves the city, _____.

ANSWER KEY

1. plans; 2. visiting; 3. going out; 4. country; 5. on, in; 6. long, take; 7. half, car; 8. does, do; 9. in, during; 10. eats, reads, watches; 11. spends, too

Grammar Builder 2

▶ 3D Grammar Builder 2 (CD 4, Track 13)

PREPOSITIONS OF LOCATION AND DIRECTION

Let's look at some common prepositions of location. The most common ones are **in** and **at**. In general, use **in** with cities, countries, buildings, rooms, and other things with walls or boundaries.

My family lives in Shanghai, in China.	
I'm watching television in my living room, in my apartment.	
The students are in the classroom.	
The juice is in the bottle, and the bottle is in the refrigerator.	

In general, use **at** with events or places that are not rooms or buildings with walls.

They're at a baseball game.	
All of my friends are at this party.	
Mrs. Jones is at a meeting now. Can I take a message?	
We're spending the day at the park.	

You'll learn more about **in** and **at** in the next Take It Further section. Here are some examples of other common prepositions of location.

The computer is <u>on</u> my desk.	
The dog is sleeping <u>under</u> the table.	
The mirror is hanging <u>over</u> the sink.	
We're <u>inside</u> the building; we're in my office.	

The Simple Present and the
Present Progressive

Object Pronouns

Commands and
Requests

Indirect Objects

We're outside (of) the building; we're waiting for a taxi.	
Philadelphia is close to New York, but Los Angeles is far from New York.	
The first floor is below the second floor, and the second floor is above the first floor.	
Thirty-seven Green Street is next to thirty-nine Green Street.	
Thirty-seven Green Street is between thirty-five Green Street and thirty-nine Green Street.	
Thirty-seven Green Street is across from thirty-six Green Street.	
The teacher stands in front of the class.	
In class, Billy sits in front of Mark, and Mark sits behind Billy.	

Beneath is another way to say **below**, and **underneath** is similar to **under**, but it means covered by (water, snow, the earth). **Opposite** is another way to say **across from**. **Near** means the same thing as **close to**.

The first floor is beneath the second floor.	
It's winter, so the grass is underneath the snow.	
Thirty-seven Green Street is opposite thirty-six Green Street.	

Prepositions of Location
and Direction

We can walk to the restaurant; it's near our house.	

Beside is similar to **next to**. **By** is similar to **near**. **Along** means next to something, but it's used with things that are long (rivers, roads).

We're sitting beside the pool, enjoying the sun.	
The house is by the lake.	
We're walking in the park, along the river.	

Now let's look at some common prepositions of direction or movement. The most common and generic one is **to**.

We're driving to the airport tomorrow morning.	
The kids walk to school because the school is close to our house.	

Toward is similar to **to**, but it means in the general direction of. **From** is the opposite of **to**.

Don't throw the ball toward the house!	
We're flying from London to Delhi.	

Into is similar to **in**, but it specifies direction, not location. **Out of** is the opposite of **into**.

I'm walking into the building now; I see the elevators.	
I'm walking out of the building now; I see the taxis.	

The Simple Present and the
Present Progressive

Object Pronouns

Commands and
Requests

Indirect Objects

Onto is similar to **on**, but it specifies direction, not location. **Off (of)** is the opposite of **onto**.

The cat is jumping <u>off of</u> the floor and <u>onto</u> the chair.	

Down to and **up to** are opposites. Use **down to** with things that are lower or below you, and **up to** with things that are higher or above you.

Go <u>down to</u> the cellar and get a bottle of wine.	
Go <u>up to</u> the seventeenth floor by elevator.	

Through, past, and **around** are other common prepositions of movement or direction. Use **through** with closed spaces that have a beginning and an end, like tunnels. If you go **past** something, you do not stop at it. If you go **around** something, you do not go through it.

Drive <u>through</u> the tunnel to get across the river.	
I always look in the window when I walk <u>past</u> the shoe store.	
This road goes <u>around</u> the lake.	

You can also use **around** to mean that you don't have a specific destination or direction.

We're driving <u>around</u> the city, but we can't find your street.	
They like to walk <u>around</u> the store and see all of the different clothes.	

Take It Further
MORE ON IN AND AT

In and at are difficult prepositions, and they have many different uses. In general, use in with buildings. But use at with public buildings and places where you typically do something specific.

We're eating at a great new restaurant this weekend.	
Barbara is a nurse; she works at the hospital.	
You can buy stamps at the post office, get books at the library, and buy milk at the convenience store.	
It's Sunday morning, so they're at church.	

Notice that in and at can be used with the same places, with slightly different meanings. These two examples use in, and they mean literally inside the restaurant or house.

I'm in the restaurant. I'm sitting down, reading the menu.	
We're in our friends' house. We're in their living room.	

These two examples use at. They don't specifically mean inside the building. You can be at a place when you're not literally inside it.

I'm at the restaurant. I'm waiting for you on the sidewalk.	

The Simple Present and the
Present Progressive

Object Pronouns

Commands and
Requests

Indirect Objects

We're at our friends' house. We're swimming in their pool.	

Use **at** with tables, desks, and other places where you typically stand or sit to do something specific. **At** is similar to **next to** in this sense.

We're all at the table, so we can eat.	
I'm at my desk. I'm writing a letter.	
John is standing at the bar in the restaurant.	

✎ Work Out 2

Choose the best preposition.

1. We're spending the weekend_____our friends' house.

   a. toward

   b. at

   c. around

   d. above

2. The letter C is_____B and D in the alphabet.

   a. in front of

   b. behind

   c. beneath

   d. between

Intermediate English

3. Philadelphia is not very_____ New York.

   a. out of

   b. toward

   c. far from

   d. from

4. Come_____ my office and sit down.

   a. into

   b. around

   c. off of

   d. off of

5. There's a beautiful picture on the wall_____ the couch.

   a. under

   b. over

   c. through

   d. along

6. My car is on the street_____ my apartment.

   a. inside

   b. along

   c. in front of

   d. up to

7. Jack's shoes are_____ his bed.

   a. above

b. **onto**

c. **under**

d. **inside**

8. Kids, go_____ your bedrooms and make your beds.

a. **past**

b. **toward**

c. **underneath**

d. **up to**

9. You have to walk_____ the bedroom to get to the bathroom.

a. **through**

b. **along**

c. **onto**

d. **above**

10. We live_____ the beach, so we go there very often.

a. **toward**

b. **by**

c. **along**

d. **outside of**

11. I don't like to sit_____ tall people at the movies, because I can't see.

a. **in front of**

b. **next to**

c. **behind**

d. **opposite**

12. Hurry up! Get_____ the shower and get dressed!

    a. **off of**

    b. **out of**

    c. **onto**

    d. **inside**

ANSWER KEY
1. b; 2. d; 3. c; 4. a; 5. b; 6. c; 7. c; 8. d; 9. a; 10. b; 11. c; 12. b

✎ Drive It Home

Choose either **say** or **tell** to complete the sentence.

1. I_____ good morning to the teacher.

2. We always_____ hello to Mr. Blake.

3. What do you_____ to Mr. Blake?

4. You_____ "yes" too much.

5. We_____ "no" sometimes.

6. Don't_____ me the end of the story.

7. _____ it to them.

8. We always_____ our parents the truth.

9. What do we_____ them?

10. They_____ the teacher their names.

ANSWER KEY
1-5 all say; 6-10 all tell

The Simple Present and the
Present Progressive

Object Pronouns

Commands and
Requests

Indirect Objects

How Did You Do?

Let's see how you did in this lesson. By now, you should know:

□ how to use the double object construction (**give Mary/her a book**) (Still unsure? Jump back to page 43.)

□ the difference between **say** and **tell** (Still unsure? Jump back to page 45.)

□ the most common prepositions of location (**at, in**) and direction (**to, toward**) (Still unsure? Jump back to page 49.)

✎ Word Recall

Let's review the prepositions you learned in this lesson. Circle which preposition best completes the sentence.

1. We drove (**under/through**) the tunnel to get across the river.

2. Go (**up to/over**) the seventh floor by elevator.

3. Walk (**toward/off**) the park.

4. Take the pie (**off/out of**) the oven.

5. It's somewhere (**around/toward**) here.

6. We're driving (**from/to**) Boston to New York.

7. He is going (**along/into**) the office.

8. The park is (**by/along**) the school.

9. My shoes are (**underneath/outside**) the table.

10. Go (**inside/under**) the building when it rains.

11. Mary is (**on/at**) the park.

12. We are (**in/at**) the car.

ANSWER KEY

1. We drove <u>through</u> the tunnel to get across the river. 2. Go <u>up to</u> the seventh floor by elevator. 3. Walk <u>toward</u> the park. 4. Take the pie <u>out of</u> the oven. 5. It's somewhere <u>around</u> here. 6. We're driving <u>from</u> Boston to New York. 7. He is going <u>into</u> the office. 8. The park is <u>by</u> the school. 9. My shoes are <u>underneath</u> the table. 10. Go <u>inside</u> the building when it rains. 11. Mary is <u>at</u> the park. 12. We are <u>in</u> the car.

Lesson 4: Conversations

In this lesson you'll learn:

☐ indefinite pronouns (someone, something, anyone, anything, and so on)

☐ how to use the and a/an in a variety of situations

Conversation 1

▶ 4A Conversation 1 (CD 4, Track 14)

How's Life? Andrea and Steven are good friends. They have busy lives, and don't see each other very often. They run into each other at a supermarket. Listen in.

Andrea:	Steven! Hey! How are you?
Steven:	Oh, hi, Andrea. Long time no see! I'm good. How are you?
Andrea:	I can't complain. Busy, but good. So, how's life?
Steven:	Well, let's see . . . our house is a disaster area. We're renovating the kitchen and one bathroom, so everything is a mess.
Andrea:	The kitchen and a bathroom at the same time? What renovations are you making?
Steven:	Well, Laura and I want new appliances, so we're getting a new refrigerator, a new oven and stove top, a new microwave, a new sink and dishwasher, and new cabinets. Especially new cabinets. We can't stand our old ones. Laura really hates them!

The Simple Present and the
Present Progressive

Object Pronouns

Commands and
Requests

Indirect Objects

Andrea:	Wow, that's a lot. And what about the bathroom?
Steven:	Well, I hate the tiles in the bathroom, so we're getting new tiles. Along with a new shower and bathtub, new toilet, and all of that.
Andrea:	So it's a compromise? You're giving Laura new kitchen cabinets and she's giving you new bathroom tiles?
Steven:	Ha, well, something like that. And how are you doing? How are Jack and the kids?
Andrea:	Everyone's doing well. But Jack is really busy at work. He's working on an important new project, so he gets home late very often. Some evenings I don't see him until eight or nine. He needs to hire someone to help him.
Steven:	That's hard. And how's work for you?
Andrea:	It's good. I'm busy, too, but we have our weekends, at least. Matthew has soccer, and Mary is taking piano lessons, so Jack or I drive them back and forth.
Steven:	It sounds like the weekends are pretty busy, too!
Andrea:	Yeah, I guess so. Speaking of which, I should get going. I have a lot of errands to run today. Say hi to Laura for me.
Steven:	Of course. And don't forget to say hello to Jack.
Andrea:	I will. Take care, Steven. Good seeing you.
Steven:	See you soon, I hope.

✎ Conversation Practice 1

Answer the following questions about Conversation 1.

1. Which rooms are Steven and Laura renovating?

_____

2. What new appliances are they getting for the kitchen?

_____

3. Do they like their old cabinets?

4. What does Steven hate about the bathroom?

5. What is Andrea's husband Jack working on?

6. Does he get home early or late?

7. What does Matthew, Andrea's son, do during the weekend?

8. What musical instrument is Mary, Andrea's daughter, learning?

ANSWER KEY

1. They're renovating the kitchen and the bathroom. 2. They're getting a new refrigerator, a new oven and stove top, a new microwave, and a new dishwasher. 3. No, they hate/can't stand their old cabinets. 4. He hates the tiles in the bathroom. 5. He's working on an important new project. 6. He gets home late very often. 7. He plays soccer. 8. She's learning the piano.

Grammar Builder 1

▶ 4B Grammar Builder 1 (CD 4, Track 15)

INDEFINITE AND OTHER PRONOUNS

Definite pronouns (I, you, he, her, us, they, etc.) refer to definite, specific people or things. Indefinite pronouns do not refer to definite, specific people or things. The most common indefinite pronouns that refer to people end in –one or –body, and the most common indefinite pronouns that refer to things end in –thing.

The Simple Present and the
Present Progressive
Object Pronouns

Commands and
Requests
Indirect Objects

Somebody/Someone and Something

Use **somebody** or **someone** to refer to a person who you don't know, or a person who is not specific. Use **something** to refer to a thing that you don't know or that is not specific.

Jack is too busy at work. He needs to hire someone to help him.	
I hear somebody in front of the house, but I don't know who it is.	
You need something to carry those books, maybe a bag or a box.	

Nobody/No one and Nothing

The negative of **someone** is **no one**, and the negative of **somebody** is **nobody**. The negative of **something** is **nothing**.

The house is empty; there is no one in it.	
Nobody wants to work on Saturday until ten o'clock at night!	
There's nothing in the refrigerator. We need to buy food.	

Everybody/Everyone and Everything

Use **everybody** or **everyone** to mean "all people." Use **everything** to mean "all things."

It's Bill's birthday, so he knows everyone at the party. They're all his friends.	

Everybody in the class speaks English very well. They're all great students.	
Everything in this store is so expensive! I don't have enough money.	

Anybody/Anyone and **Anything**

Use **anybody**, **anyone**, and **anything** in questions and in negative sentences.

–Do you know anybody here? –No, I don't know anybody here.	
–Is there anyone home right now? –No, there isn't anyone home right now.	
–Do you have anything in your bag? –No, I don't have anything in my bag.	

But remember that you use **somebody**, **someone**, and **something** in positive sentences.

–Do you know anybody here? –Yes, I know somebody here.	
–Is there anyone home right now? –Yes, there's someone home right now.	
–Do you have anything in your bag? –Yes, I have something in my bag.	

The Simple Present and the
Present Progressive

Object Pronouns

Commands and
Requests

Indirect Objects

✎ Work Out 1

Fill in the blanks with someone, something, no one, nothing, everyone, everything, anyone, or anything.

1. Do you know_____ in Professor Hill's English class?

2. _____ on the menu at this restaurant is delicious!

3. _____ in my family speaks French. We all speak English and Spanish.

4. I need_____ for a headache. Do you have any aspirin or ibuprofen?

5. Bill is bringing_____ to the restaurant tonight, but we don't know who it is.

6. You're so busy! Can I do_____ to help you?

7. The room is completely empty. There's_____ in it.

8. _____ at the beach is swimming or lying in the sun.

ANSWER KEY
1. anyone; 2. Everything; 3. No one; 4. something; 5. someone; 6. anything; 7. nothing; 8. Everyone

⏏ Conversation 2

▶ 4C Conversation 2 (CD 4, Track 16)

It's Friday. Nicole and Geraldine work for the same company, and they meet in the break room. Listen in as they talk about their weekend plans.

Nicole: What a week!

Geraldine: I know! It's crazy. But at least it's Friday. What are your plans for the weekend? Are you and Rob doing anything special?

Nicole: We're visiting my parents at their lake house. They have a place up on Pleasant Lake, in the mountains.

Geraldine:	Nice! How far is it?
Nicole:	Not too far. It takes about two hours to get to the house by car. We're leaving early tomorrow morning, so we should be there before lunch.
Geraldine:	A two hour drive? Do the kids get bored?
Nicole:	Not with the video games and DVD player and music and everything else!
Geraldine:	Kids love gadgets. Do you remember when we were kids? We had nothing like that!
Nicole:	No. They know the rules. They can play video games in the car, but when we're at the house, they have to go outside and play in the woods or swim in the lake. Luckily they love swimming, so they forget about all the electronic toys.
Geraldine:	So, you'll spend a relaxing weekend in the country. That sounds really nice.
Nicole:	Yes, I'm looking forward to it. How about you? Do you have any plans?
Geraldine:	Unfortunately we're not relaxing this weekend! We're painting the living room and one of the bedrooms.
Nicole:	That doesn't sound relaxing at all!
Geraldine:	It's not that bad. John and I enjoy painting, and we're both tired of the colors on the walls now.
Nicole:	And that's your whole weekend?
Geraldine:	No, tomorrow night we're going to John's sister's place. She's cooking us dinner, after a long day of painting.
Nicole:	Well, that sounds better. Do you see John's sister often?
Geraldine:	She lives in town, so we see her pretty often. She visits us at our place, or we visit her. Sometimes we go out to dinner together, or watch a movie. And on Sunday, she's showing some of her new paintings at an art gallery in town, so we're going there for a few hours.
Nicole:	More paint?

The Simple Present and the
Present Progressive
Object Pronouns

Commands and
Requests
Indirect Objects

Geraldine: That's funny, yes, more paint. But we're only looking at the paint on Sunday, and we really love art galleries.

Nicole: Well, enjoy the painting on Saturday, and the paintings on Sunday.

Geraldine: Thanks. And you enjoy your weekend at the lake house. Say hi to Rob for me.

✎ Conversation Practice 2

Answer the following questions about Conversation 2.

1. What are Rob and Nicole doing over the weekend?

   _____

2. How long does it take to get there by car?

   _____

3. What do the kids do during the drive?

   _____

4. Can the kids play video games at the lake house?

   _____

5. Are John and Geraldine relaxing this weekend?

   _____

6. Where are they going on Saturday night?

   _____

7. How often do John and Geraldine see John's sister?

   _____

8. What are they doing on Sunday?

ANSWER KEY

1. They're visiting Nicole's parents at their lake house. 2. It takes two hours to get there by car. 3. They play video games and watch DVDs. 4. No, they have to play outside or swim. 5. No, they're painting their living room and one of their bedrooms. 6. They're going to John's sister's place for dinner. 7. They see her pretty often. 8. They're going to an art gallery to see some of John's sister's new paintings.

Grammar Builder 2

(▶) 4D Grammar Builder 2 (CD 4, Track 17)

DEFINITE ARTICLES, INDEFINITE ARTICLES, AND "BARE" NOUNS

In Lesson 4 of *Essential English*, you learned how to use the definite article (**the**) and the indefinite article (**a/an**). Let's review and expand your knowledge. Remember that in a conversation, when you talk about something for the first time, you usually use **a/an**. After that, use **the**.

We're going to an art gallery this weekend. The gallery is on Orchard Street.	
We're seeing a movie next week. The movie is playing at City Cinemas.	
We're buying a new couch. The couch is very big and comfortable.	

Use **a/an** with something that is indefinite, non-specific, or general.

Many people have a dog or a cat.	

The Simple Present and the
Present Progressive

Object Pronouns

Commands and
Requests

Indirect Objects

An apartment in New York City is expensive.	
I always love to read a good book.	

Use a/an if the person you're talking to doesn't know about the person, place or thing you're talking about.

–I'm buying a new computer this weekend.
–What kind of computer is it?

–We're visiting a good friend this weekend.
–Oh really? Who is it?

Use the with definite or specific things.

The dog in the house next door is very big.	
The apartment above us is bigger than our apartment.	
The book on my desk is new.	

Use the with famous things that everyone knows.

The Statue of Liberty is in New York.	
The Grand Canyon is very beautiful.	
The Great Wall of China is very old.	

Use the if the person you're speaking to knows about the person, place, or thing that you're speaking about.

–How are your new courses?
–The English literature course is great, but the chemistry course is hard.

–Who are those kids over there?
–The boy is our nephew, and the girl is our niece.

Count nouns are nouns that you can count: one apple, two apples; one train, two trains. To make general statements about count nouns, use a/an with the singular, or use a "bare" plural – a plural noun without any article.

An apple is red, yellow, or green. Apples are red, yellow, or green.	
A train is long and fast. Trains are long and fast.	
A dog is a great pet. Dogs are great pets.	

Noncount or mass nouns are nouns that you cannot count: water, air, sugar, flour. Do not use a/an with mass nouns.

Sugar is sweet.	
Bread has flour in it.	
There's water in my glass.	
He's drinking coffee, and she's eating fruit.	

Mass nouns normally don't have plurals. But some mass nouns can be used as count nouns: a coffee means a cup of coffee, a water means a glass of water. In this case, you can use the plural.

I'd like a coffee with sugar, and two teas, please.	
–Would you like wine with dinner? –No thanks, just three waters.	

You can use **the** with count or mass nouns, but again, **the** means that you're talking about something specific, and both you and the person you're talking to know what the noun refers to. Compare:

GENERIC/INDEFINITE	SPECIFIC/DEFINITE
Fruit is healthy for you.	The fruit on my desk is from the supermarket.
Bananas are delicious.	The bananas at this store are expensive.
An elephant is a big animal.	The elephant at the zoo is named Tembo.
Many people drink coffee in the morning.	Don't drink the coffee in that cup; it's cold.
You use flour to make bread.	The flour in my refrigerator is old.

Finally, remember how to use **some**, which you learned in Lesson 7 of Essential English. **Some** means an amount that is not specific. Use it with both mass nouns and count nouns. But with count nouns, use the plural after **some**.

I have some fruit in the refrigerator, and some bread in the drawer.	
There are some bananas in the bowl.	
I'm drinking some tea and eating some cookies.	

Some becomes **any** in questions and negative statements.

You're drinking <u>some</u> tea. You aren't drinking <u>any</u> tea. Are you drinking <u>any</u> tea?	
You want <u>some</u> sugar. You don't want <u>any</u> sugar. Do you want <u>any</u> sugar?	

But you'll also hear **some** in questions, especially when the speaker is asking about something that he or she knows exists, but the specific amount isn't important.

We have coffee, but we don't have any tea. Would you like some coffee?	
There are cookies in the kitchen. Would you like some cookies?	

Take It Further
REGULAR AND IRREGULAR PLURALS

Most plurals in English end in –s.

cup	cups
house	houses
car	cars

If the noun ends in –y, change the **y** to **i** and add –es.

university	universities
city	cities
study	studies

If the noun ends in –s, –sh, –ch, –x, or –z, add –es.

loss	losses
dish	dishes
match	matches
box	boxes
buzz	buzzes

The Simple Present and the
Present Progressive

Object Pronouns

Commands and
Requests

Indirect Objects

Some nouns that end in –o add –es in the plural, but some only add –s.

potato	potatoes
tomato	tomatoes
photo	photos
video	videos

Some nouns that end in –f change the f to v and add –es in the plural. But some keep the f and just add –s.

knife	knives
life	lives
shelf	shelves
scarf	scarves
wolf	wolves
roof	roofs
cliff	cliffs
belief	beliefs

Some nouns have the same form in the singular and plural.

deer	deer
fish	fish
sheep	sheep
shrimp	shrimp

A few nouns have irregular plurals.

person	people
man	men
woman	women
child	children
tooth	teeth

foot	feet
goose	geese
mouse	mice
ox	oxen
louse	lice

Some nouns from other languages, for example Latin or Greek, have irregular plurals. They're not all common, and many are related to science or academics.

cactus	cacti
fungus	fungi
phenomenon	phenomena
analysis	analyses
crisis	crises
nucleus	nuclei
hypothesis	hypotheses

✎ Work Out 2

Complete each sentence with a, an, the, or Ø (nothing).

1. Our neighbors are getting_____ new dog.

2. Who is_____ man with your boss?

3. I really need_____ new car!

4. I like_____ milk in my tea.

5. _____ chair in my office is not comfortable at all.

6. There's_____ apple in the tree.

The Simple Present and the
Present Progressive

Object Pronouns

Commands and
Requests

Indirect Objects

7. My shirt is made of_____ cotton.

8. _____ computers in this store are too expensive.

9. Hey look! I can see_____ boat out there on the lake.

10. We're visiting_____ Empire State Building this weekend.

11. Could I have_____ glass of orange juice, please?

12. There are_____ lions at the zoo.

13. Could I borrow_____ dollar?

14. _____ man in this photo is my father.

15. I know_____ excellent new restaurant.

ANSWER KEY
1. a; 2. the; 3. a; 4. Ø; 5. The; 6. an; 7. Ø; 8. The; 9. a; 10. the; 11. a; 12. Ø; 13. a; 14. The; 15. an

✎ Drive It Home

Choose some or any to complete the sentence.

1. You're drinking_____ water.

2. They are eating_____ cookies.

3. I want_____ sugar in my tea.

4. We have coffee. Would you like_____?

5. They're making_____ coffee.

6. You're not drinking_____ water.

7. Are they eating_____ cookies?

8. Do you want_____ sugar in your tea?

9. We have tea, but we don't have_____ coffee.

10. We aren't making_____coffee.

ANSWER KEY
1-5 all some; 6-10 all any

How Did You Do?

Let's see how you did in this lesson. By now, you should know:

☐ Indefinite pronouns (someone, something, anyone, anything, and so on) (Still unsure? Jump back to page 61.)

☐ How to use the and a/an in a variety of situations (Still unsure? Jump back to page 67.)

✎ Word Recall

Give the irregular plural for the following nouns.

1. fish _____

2. dish _____

3. goose _____

4. knife _____

5. cactus _____

6. crisis _____

7. shelf _____

8. foot _____

9. potato _____

10. person _____

The Simple Present and the
Present Progressive

Object Pronouns

Commands and
Requests

Indirect Objects

11. photo_____

12. city_____

ANSWER KEY

1. fish; 2. dishes; 3. geese; 4. knives; 5. cacti; 6. crises; 7. shelves; 8. feet; 9. potatoes; 10. people; 11. photos; 12. cities

Don't forget to practice and reinforce what you've learned by visiting **www.livinglanguage.com/languagelab** for flashcards, games, and quizzes!

Unit 1 Quiz

Let's put the most essential English words and grammar points you've learned so far to practice in a few exercises. It's important to be sure that you've mastered this material before you move on. Score yourself at the end of the review and see if you need to go back for more practice, or if you're ready to move on to Unit 2.

A. Complete the sentences with either the present progressive or the simple present form of the verb in parentheses.

1. _____ in the city next week? (you, work)

2. We_____ for our test right now. (study)

3. I always_____ the train to work. (take)

4. He_____ dinner on the table now. (put)

B. Form negative commands, both regular and polite—please don't, would you please not—from the questions below.

1. Did you take this book?

   _____

2. Are you sitting in front of the television all night?

   _____

C. Change the underlined noun to a subject or object pronoun—either direct or indirect. If a double object pronoun is possible, give both answers.

1. He is taking Mary to the theater.

   _____

2. We are giving Jim our old car.

   _____

3. Salim speaks fluent Mandarin Chinese.

   _____

4. Are you going to the movies with Amanda and Chris?

   _____

5. Justin is sending it to Elena.

   _____

D. Fill in the correct preposition of location or direction.

1. Fifty-seventh Street is_____Fifty-sixth Street and Fifty-eighth Street.

2. My mother works_____the hospital.

3. They live_____ Santa Monica.

4. They're going_____ the beach.

E. Answer the following questions with a negative indefinite pronoun.

1. Is there someone at the door?

   _____

2. Do you have anything to eat?

   _____

F. Fill in the correct article in each sentence below. If no article is needed, leave it blank.

1. _____ store on the corner sells good produce.

2. That is_____ great book.

3. Do you take_____ milk in your coffee?

ANSWER KEY
A. 1. **Are you working**; 2. **are studying**; 3. **take**; 4. **is putting**
B. 1. **Please don't take this book./Would you please not take this book?** 2. **Please don't sit in front of the television all night./Would you please not sit in front of the television all night?**
C. 1. **He is taking her to the theater.** 2. **We are giving our old car to him./We are giving him our old car.** 3. **He speaks fluent Mandarin Chinese.** 4. **Are you going to the movies with them?** 5. **Justin is sending it to her.**
D. 1. **between**; 2. **at**; 3. **in**; 4. **to**
E. 1. **There is no one at the door.** 2. **I have nothing to eat.**
F. 1. **The**; 2. **a**; 3. **Ø**

How Did You Do?

Give yourself a point for every correct answer, then use the following key to tell whether you're ready to move on:

0–7 points: It's probably a good idea to go back through the lesson again. You may be moving too quickly, or there may be too much "down time" between your contact with English. Remember that it's better to spend 30 minutes with English three or four times a week than it is to spend two or three hours just once a week.

Find a pace that's comfortable for you, and spread your contact hours out as much as you can.

8–12 points: You would benefit from a review before moving on. Go back and spend a little more time on the specific points that gave you trouble. Re-read the Grammar Builder sections that were difficult, and do the work out one more time. Don't forget about the online supplemental practice material, either. Go to **www.livinglanguage.com/languagelab** for games and quizzes that will reinforce the material from this unit.

13–17 points: Good job! There are just a few points that you could consider reviewing before moving on. If you haven't worked with the games and quizzes on **www.livinglanguage.com/languagelab**, please give them a try.

18–20 points: Great! You're ready to move on to the next unit.

 **points**

Unit 2:
Work and School

Welcome to Unit 2. This unit is all about work and school, so you'll learn important vocabulary related to the workplace, to jobs, to school, and to universities. You'll also learn how to use the simple past tense (was, went, talked), as well as the simple future (will be, will go, will talk) and the future with going to. But that's not all. We'll focus on more prepositions, such as during, before, and with, and we'll talk about the to verb form, known as the infinitive. You'll also learn how to make longer, more complex sentences with and, or, but, even though, and so on, and you'll learn how to give more information about a noun in a sentence with words like who, which, and that.

Lesson 5: Words
In this lesson you'll learn:

☐ essential vocabulary related to jobs and working

☐ how to use the simple past tense (was, went, did)

☐ basic vocabulary related to schools and universities

☐ how to use prepositions of time (during, before) and other common prepositions (with, about, etc.)

The Simple Past Tense

Adverbs and Adverbial
Phrases with –ing

Prepositions of Time and
Other Useful Prepositions

Infinitives of Purpose

Word Builder 1

▶ 5A Word Builder 1 (CD 4, Track 18)

Here is some key vocabulary that you should know for Unit 2. Let's start with vocabulary for work.

work, job, full-time job, part-time job	
company, corporation, business	
office, desk, cubicle, conference room	
schedule, calendar	
meeting, presentation, interview, report	
sales, marketing, accounting	
salary, pay, raise, promotion	
medical benefits, dental benefits	
doctor, lawyer, nurse, police officer, mail carrier	
salesperson, manager, director, secretary, assistant	
plumber, electrician, carpenter, construction worker	
butcher, baker, pharmacist	
cook, chef, waiter, waitress, server	
engineer, architect, editor, journalist	

✎ Word Practice 1

Let's practice the vocabulary you just learned. Fill in each sentence with the best word or words from Word Builder 1. Some sentences have more than one possible answer.

1. I don't have a full-time job; I only have a_____ job.

2. GE, Ford, Samsung, AT&T, and Siemens are all

   big_____.

3. The meeting is in the_____.

4. Mrs. Jackson's_____ is very full this week. Can you see her

   next week?

5. If you want to get that job, don't be late for your_____.

6. Phil's assistant is writing a_____ for him.

7. If you want more money, ask for a_____.

8. On top of your_____, you'll also get medical and dental benefits.

9. _____ work in hospitals and help doctors and patients.

10. We have no water in our apartment; we have to call a_____.

11. Go to the drugstore and give the prescription to

    the_____.

12. As soon as we get to the table, the_____ gives us the menu.

13. We need an_____ to design the building.

14. Bob's a_____; he works for a big newspaper.

ANSWER KEY
1. **part-time**; 2. **corporations** or **companies**; 3. **conference room**; 4. **schedule** or **calendar**; 5. **interview**; 6. **report**; 7. **raise**; 8. **salary** or **pay**; 9. **Nurses**; 10. **plumber**; 11. **pharmacist**; 12. **server** or **waiter** or **waitress**; 13. **architect**; 14. **journalist**

The Simple Past Tense

Adverbs and Adverbial
Phrases with –ing

Prepositions of Time and
Other Useful Prepositions

Infinitives of Purpose

Grammar Builder 1

5B Grammar Builder 1 (CD 4, Track 19)

THE SIMPLE PAST TENSE

In Unit 1 you reviewed the simple present (goes, walks) and the present progressive (is going, is walking). Now let's look at the simple past (went, walked). The simple past expresses actions in the past; you can use it with expressions like yesterday, last week, last year, in 2005, before now, earlier, and so on.

With regular verbs, simply add –ed to form the simple past:

SIMPLE PRESENT	SIMPLE PAST
work	worked
turn	turned
listen	listened

I worked from nine o'clock to five thirty yesterday.	
We listened to music last night.	

If the verb ends in a consonant followed by –e, just add –d:

SIMPLE PRESENT	SIMPLE PAST
like	liked
hope	hoped
love	loved

She liked the new restaurant very much.	
The kids loved their Christmas presents.	

If the verb ends in a consonant followed by –y, the past tense ends in –ied. But if it ends in a vowel followed by –y (for example –ay or –oy), keep the y and add –ed.

SIMPLE PRESENT	SIMPLE PAST
copy	copied
study	studied
play	played
enjoy	enjoyed

Sarah studied all weekend for her test.	
Their friends enjoyed the party very much.	

With many short verbs that end in a single consonant, double the consonant before adding –ed.

SIMPLE PRESENT	SIMPLE PAST
stop	stopped
beg	begged
trip	tripped

The bus stopped in front of my apartment early this morning.	
Jack tripped over his shoes on the bedroom floor.	

Many common verbs have irregular past tense forms that you have to memorize. Usually there is a vowel change in the simple past, but often there are other changes. There are a lot of irregular verbs in English. In this section, we'll only look at the more common ones. See the Grammar Summary for a more complete list.

The Simple Past Tense

Adverbs and Adverbial
Phrases with –ing

Prepositions of Time and
Other Useful Prepositions

Infinitives of Purpose

Be is the only verb with two forms in the past tense: (**I, he, she, it**) **was** and (**you, we, they**) **were**.

SIMPLE PRESENT	SIMPLE PAST
am, is	was
are	were

I was in the office until eight o'clock last night.	
They were at their friends' house last week.	

All other verbs, both regular and irregular, have one past tense form. Let's divide the most useful irregular verbs into small groups with similar changes. Many simple past tense forms end in –t, sometimes with a vowel change, sometimes without. The very common verb go changes completely into went.

SIMPLE PRESENT	SIMPLE PAST
go	went
build	built
feel	felt
keep	kept
leave	left
lose	lost
mean	meant
meet	met
send	sent
sleep	slept
spend	spent

We went to a great new restaurant this weekend, but we spent too much money.	

She felt tired all evening, and slept ten hours last night.	

Several verbs use the endings **–ought** or **–aught** in the simple past tense.

SIMPLE PRESENT	SIMPLE PAST
bring	brought
buy	bought
fight	fought
think	thought
catch	caught
teach	taught

Jack brought me to a great store at the mall, where I bought a new shirt.	
Who taught you how to speak Russian?	

A lot of common verbs end in **–w** in the past tense.

SIMPLE PRESENT	SIMPLE PAST
blow	blew
draw	drew
fly	flew
know	knew
see	saw
throw	threw
grow	grew

The teacher saw that no one knew the answer.	
They flew in from London yesterday.	

The Simple Past Tense

Adverbs and Adverbial
Phrases with –ing

Prepositions of Time and
Other Useful Prepositions

Infinitives of Purpose

Some common verbs have the same form in the simple present and simple past. Notice that **read** is pronounced like **reed** in the present tense, but like **red** in the past tense. All of the other verbs in this list are spelled and pronounced the same in both tenses.

SIMPLE PRESENT	SIMPLE PAST
read	read
cost	cost
cut	cut
hit	hit
hurt	hurt
let	let
put	put
quit	quit
shut	shut

I read this book in one day.	
She put on her hat and shut the door.	

Here are some common verbs that have a long **o** (as in **so**) sound in the past tense.

SIMPLE PRESENT	SIMPLE PAST
break	broke
choose	chose
freeze	froze
ride	rode
sell	sold
speak	spoke
tell	told
wake	woke
write	wrote

I wrote three e-mails and then spoke to my boss.	
I woke up sick and chose to stay home today.	

Many common irregular verbs have a short a sound (as in bad) in the past tense.

SIMPLE PRESENT	SIMPLE PAST
have	had
drink	drank
begin	began
ring	rang
run	ran
sing	sang
sit	sat
swim	swam

We sat down at the bar and drank a glass of wine.	
They had a great time until it began to rain.	

Here are some common verbs that have an oo (as in look) sound in the past tense.

SIMPLE PRESENT	SIMPLE PAST
take	took
stand	stood
understand	understood

I took a shower and left for work.	
He understood the question.	

Unit 2 Lesson 5: Words   89

The Simple Past Tense

Adverbs and Adverbial
Phrases with –ing

Prepositions of Time and
Other Useful Prepositions

Infinitives of Purpose

Here are some common verbs that have a long **a** (as in **day**) sound in the past tense.

SIMPLE PRESENT	SIMPLE PAST
eat	ate
come	came
give	gave
make	made
pay	paid

They came over at seven, and we ate at eight thirty.	
The kids made a birthday card and gave it to their mother.	

And here are some other common verbs in the simple present and simple past tense. Notice the vowels and other spelling changes.

SIMPLE PRESENT	SIMPLE PAST
do	did
get	got
fall	fell
find	found
forget	forgot
hang	hung
hear	heard
hide	hid
say	said
wear	wore
win	won

He said that he forgot her name.	

We did a lot of exercise and then got tired.	

Remember that both questions and the negative in the simple present use **does/ do**. In the simple past, questions and the negative use **did**. Use the basic form of the verb with **did**: **He <u>went</u>** becomes **did he <u>go</u>?** in questions and **he did not <u>go</u>** in the negative.

–Did he go to the supermarket? –No, he didn't go to the supermarket; he went to the convenience store.	
–Did you see your sister? –No, I didn't see my sister, but I saw my brother.	
–How many nights did your guests stay? –They didn't stay long. They only stayed one night.	

Take It Further
HOW TO PRONOUNCE –(E)D

The past tense ending –(e)d has three different pronunciations: /t/, /d/, and /id/. Pronounce it as /t/ after **k, p, s, ch, sh**, and **f** sounds. This includes **x**, which is pronounced /ks/, so it ends in /s/.

-(E)D PRONOUNCED AS /T/	
liked, stopped, kissed, watched, finished, laughed, relaxed, fixed	

The Simple Past Tense

Adverbs and Adverbial
Phrases with –ing

Prepositions of Time and
Other Useful Prepositions

Infinitives of Purpose

Pronounce –(e)d as /id/ after **t** and **d** sounds. Notice that /id/ is a new syllable added to the verb.

–(E)D **PRONOUNCED AS /ID/**	
decided, guarded, wanted, waited, tasted	

Pronounce –(e)d as /d/ everywhere else, including after vowel sounds.

–(E)D **PRONOUNCED AS /D/**	
played, stayed, enjoyed, cleaned, feared, smelled, formed, grabbed, saved	

 Work Out 1

Rewrite the following sentences, changing the simple present or the present progressive to the simple past. Use the words in parentheses, following the example.

Example: I am walking to work tomorrow. (… yesterday)
Answer: **I walked to work yesterday.**

1. My parents are staying with us this weekend. (… **last weekend**)

2. I write a lot of reports at work every week. (… **last week**)

3. We're studying French literature this semester. (… **last semester**)

4. She talks on the phone every day. (… **yesterday**)

5. Every Saturday morning we get up early and go jogging. (**Last Saturday morning** …)

6. We work from nine to five every Monday. (… **last Monday**)

7. They're leaving the house at seven and catching a nine thirty flight tomorrow.

(… yesterday)

8. Next week Sonia is reading a book and then she's taking a test. (Last week …).

9. Tomorrow night we're eating dinner at a restaurant and then watching a movie.

(Last night …)

10. Every day Jill comes to work early and gets home late. (Yesterday …)

11. Bill drinks orange juice and eats an egg for breakfast every morning. (…

yesterday morning)

12. This week John is home sick, so he's sleeping late every morning. (Last week …)

ANSWER KEY

1. My parents stayed with us last weekend. 2. I wrote a lot of reports at work last week. 3. We studied French literature last semester. 4. She talked on the phone yesterday. 5. Last Saturday morning we got up early and went jogging. 6. We worked from nine to five last Monday. 7. They left the house at seven and caught a nine thirty flight yesterday. 8. Last week Sonia read a book and then she took a test. 9. Last night we ate dinner at a restaurant and then watched a movie. 10. Yesterday Jill came to work early and got home late. 11. Bill drank orange juice and ate an egg for breakfast yesterday morning. 12. Last week John was home sick, so he slept late every morning.

Word Builder 2

▶ 5C Word Builder 2 (CD 4, Track 20)

Here is some key vocabulary for Unit 2 related to school.

school, elementary school, middle school, high school, college, university	
teacher, student, professor	
class, course, seminar, lecture	
classroom, lecture hall, desk, textbook	

The Simple Past Tense

Adverbs and Adverbial
Phrases with –ing

Prepositions of Time and
Other Useful Prepositions

Infinitives of Purpose

subjects: math, science, biology, chemistry, physics, history, literature, art	
test, exam, grade, report card, transcript	
diploma, degree, bachelor's degree, master's degree, doctorate	
campus, dormitory, cafeteria, dining hall	

✎ Word Practice 2

Let's practice the vocabulary you just learned. Fill in each sentence with the best word or words from Word Builder 2. Some sentences have more than one possible answer.

1. Right before college, kids go to_____.

2. The_____ stands in front of the students and teaches.

3. Every_____ in the class works very hard.

4. Last semester I took a Spanish literature_____.

5. _____ was always his favorite subject; he loved algebra, geometry, and calculus.

6. We're taking an English_____ course, so we're reading a lot of Shakespeare.

7. Biology, chemistry, and physics are all fields of_____.

8. We learned about Monet, Van Gogh, and Renoir in our_____ history class.

9. I had an_____ yesterday, so I studied for it all weekend.

10. Did you get a good_____ on your test?

11. What kind of_____ did you get, a bachelor's, a master's,

   or a doctorate?

12. A typical college_____ has lots of dormitories, a cafeteria, a dining

   hall, and lots of classrooms and offices.

ANSWER KEY

1. high school; 2. teacher or professor; 3. student; 4. course or class or seminar; 5. Math; 6. literature; 7. science; 8. art; 9. exam; 10. grade; 11.degree; 12. campus

Grammar Builder 2

▶ 5D Grammar Builder 2 (CD 5, Track 1)

PREPOSITIONS OF TIME AND OTHER USEFUL PREPOSITIONS

In Lesson 3 you learned some useful prepositions of location and direction or movement. Now let's look at some more common prepositions, starting with prepositions of time. Remember that you use **at** with times, **on** with days and dates, and **in** with months, years, and seasons.

Class starts <u>at</u> one ten <u>in</u> the afternoon.	
She has class <u>on</u> Mondays and Wednesdays.	
We start school <u>on</u> August 25th.	
School starts <u>in</u> September, and ends <u>in</u> late spring.	
She got her doctorate <u>in</u> 2009.	

The Simple Past Tense

Adverbs and Adverbial
Phrases with –ing

Prepositions of Time and
Other Useful Prepositions

Infinitives of Purpose

Use **in** with **morning, afternoon,** and **evening,** but use **at** with **night.**

Do you go to the gym in the morning or in the afternoon?	
I love to read at night.	

Here are examples of the common prepositions **before, after,** and **during.**
Following means the same thing as **after.**

The movie started at eight, and we ate at seven; we ate before the movie.	
The movie ended at eight, and we ate at eight thirty; we ate after the movie.	
Don't talk during the movie! It's rude.	
Everyone can ask questions following the presentation.	

From and **until** are also used with time expressions.

I was in class from one o'clock until three o'clock. Class lasted two hours.	
It usually snows in Chicago from December until March.	

Now let's look at some other common prepositions. **With** is similar to **and,** and its opposite is **without.**

I'd like some coffee with milk and sugar.	
We went to the movies with our friends.	

I don't want sugar in my tea. I want tea without sugar.	

You saw the preposition for in Lesson 2, with indirect objects. For has many uses in English. Here are some of the most important ones.

Jill is getting a computer for her husband.	
I'm buying groceries for my mother.	
We had sushi for lunch.	
What did you get for your birthday?	
We bought the car for five thousand dollars.	
Take aspirin for a headache.	
Jason talked about his problems for hours.	

Another meaning of for is in agreement with. If you like an idea, you are for it. If you don't like an idea, you are against it.

The president said he is for spending cuts, but against tax increases.	

A common idiomatic expression is to have something against (a person or thing). If you have something against Bill, you don't like Bill. If you don't have anything against Bill, you don't dislike him. If you're all for Bill, you really like him.

I have nothing against Chinese food. Let's go to Hunan Garden for dinner tonight.	
No, we can't. Sheila's all for Thai food, so we're going to Siam Thai Palace.	

The Simple Past Tense

Adverbs and Adverbial
Phrases with –ing

Prepositions of Time and
Other Useful Prepositions

Infinitives of Purpose

About refers to the subject of something, for example a book or conversation.

I'm reading a book about the history of Moscow.	
We talked about politics for hours!	

Let's look at the meanings of among, besides, because of, despite, and except.

There are twenty students in the class, but only three are American. Among the twenty students in the class, only three are American.	
My favorite foods are Italian, Thai, and Indian. Besides Italian and Thai, I really like Indian food.	
The weather is bad, so we're not having a game today. Because of the bad weather, we're not having a game today.	
The weather is bad today, but we're still having a game today. Despite the bad weather, we're having a game today.	
Brian is the only short player on the team. All of the players except Brian are tall.	

✎ Work Out 2

Choose the best preposition.

1. Class starts at ten in the morning, so let's have breakfast at

   nine,_____class.

   a. **during**

   b. **before**

   c. **in**

   d. **after**

2. They never work_____ Saturdays or Sundays.

   a. **in**

   b. **at**

   c. **of**

   d. **on**

3. Is your birthday_____ November or December?

   a. **in**

   b. **on**

   c. **over**

   d. **among**

4. It gets cold_____ night up here in the mountains.

   a. **in**

   b. **on**

   c. **at**

   d. **of**

The Simple Past Tense

Adverbs and Adverbial
Phrases with –ing

Prepositions of Time and
Other Useful Prepositions

Infinitives of Purpose

5. It's two o'clock_____ the morning! Go to bed!

   a. on

   b. at

   c. in

   d. of

6. _____ his morning shower, he shaves and gets dressed.

   a. After

   b. Before

   c. During

   d. Despite

7. We never speak English_____ our Spanish class.

   a. at

   b. among

   c. during

   d. between

8. It rained_____ Saturday until yesterday.

   a. on

   b. out of

   c. until

   d. from

9. You paid one hundred dollars _____ a book? That's expensive!

   a. **for**

   b. **against**

   c. **on**

   d. **in**

10. Our teacher is _____ cell phones in class. He hates it if one rings in class.

    a. **opposite**

    b. **against**

    c. **for**

    d. **despite**

11. What are you writing _____ ?

    a. **over**

    b. **under**

    c. **about**

    d. **among**

12. I bought the car _____ the high price.

    a. **despite**

    b. **of**

    c. **except**

    d. **among**

ANSWER KEY

1. b; 2. d; 3. a; 4. c; 5. c; 6. a; 7. c; 8. d; 9. a; 10. b; 11. c; 12. a

The Simple Past Tense

Adverbs and Adverbial
Phrases with –ing

Prepositions of Time and
Other Useful Prepositions

Infinitives of Purpose

✎ Drive It Home

Fill in the blank with the correct preposition of time (**in**, **on**, or **at**) to complete the sentence.

1. Class starts_____ ten.

2. We have dinner_____ seven-thirty.

3. I go to the gym_____ night.

4. I go to the gym_____ the morning.

5. I go to school_____ the spring.

6. They graduated_____ 2008.

7. We start school_____ September.

8. We start school_____ September 1st.

9. We have class_____ Monday.

10. What are you doing_____ Friday the 31st?

ANSWER KEY
1-3 all **at**; 4-7 all **in**; 8-10 all **on**

How Did You Do?

Let's see how you did in this lesson. By now, you should know:

☐ essential vocabulary related to jobs and working
(Still unsure? Jump back to page 82.)

☐ how to use the simple past tense (**was, went, did**)
(Still unsure? Jump back to page 84.)

☐ basic vocabulary related to schools and universities
(Still unsure? Jump back to page 93.)

☐ how to use prepositions of time (**during, before**) and other common prepositions
(**with, about**, etc.) (Still unsure? Jump back to page 95.)

✎ Word Recall

Match the words in the left column to the words in the right column that are most
closely related.

1. **plumber**	a. **raise**
2. **school**	b. **professor**
3. **salary**	c. **degree**
4. **math**	d. **electrician**
5. **teacher**	e. **physics**
6. **manager**	f. **college**
7. **diploma**	g. **assistant**
8. **schedule**	h. **calendar**

ANSWER KEY
1. d ; 2. f; 3. a; 4. e; 5. b; 6. g; 7. c; 8. h

Lesson 6: Phrases

In this lesson you'll learn:

☐ how to use adverbs and adverbial phrases with –ing

☐ how to use infinitives to express purpose (**to go, in order to go**)

The Simple Past Tense

Adverbs and Adverbial
Phrases with –ing

Prepositions of Time and
Other Useful Prepositions

Infinitives of Purpose

Phrase Builder 1

6A Phrase Builder 1 (CD 5, Track 2)

to commute to work by car/bus/ train	
to apply for a job	
to have an interview	
to get a job	
to hire someone for a job	
to have a meeting	
to work late	
to write a report	
to check voicemail	
to give a presentation	
to get a promotion	
to get a raise	
to quit	
to fire someone from a job	
to retire	

✎ Phrase Practice 1

Fill in the blank with the best word from Phrase Builder 1.

1. Frank_____ to work by train every day.

2. John has no money. He really needs to get a_____.

3. Frank_____ for a job last week, but he's still waiting to hear from them.

4. You have an_____ tomorrow? Dress professionally and make

    a good impression!

5. They have no assistant, so they need to_____ someone for that job.

6. The sales department has a_____ today at one o'clock in the

    conference room.

7. Joe has too much to do this week, so he's working_____ again tomorrow

    night.

8. Cheryl wrote a_____ and gave it to her boss.

9. I checked my_____, but no one left any messages.

10. I'm working very hard, so I hope I get a_____.

11. Walt found a new job, so he_____ his old one.

12. Many people_____ at age sixty-five.

ANSWER KEY
1. commutes; 2. job; 3. applied; 4. interview; 5. hire; 6. meeting; 7. late; 8. report; 9. voicemail; 10. promotion or raise; 11. quit; 12. retire

Grammar Builder 1
▶ 6B Grammar Builder 1 (CD 5, Track 3)

ADVERBS AND ADVERBIAL PHRASES WITH –ING

Remember that adjectives describe people, places, or things. Adverbs usually describe verbs, and they tell you how, when, or how much/to what degree something is done. But adverbs can also modify adjectives (very happy) or other adverbs (really quickly).

ADJECTIVE	ADVERB
Mark is a slow reader.	Mark reads slowly.

The Simple Past Tense

Adverbs and Adverbial
Phrases with –ing

Prepositions of Time and
Other Useful Prepositions

Infinitives of Purpose

In the example with an adjective, slow describes Mark as a reader. But in the example with an adverb, slowly describes how Mark reads.

A lot of adverbs in English end in –ly, which is added to the adjective.

ADJECTIVE	ADVERB
quick: Sue is quick.	quickly: Sue did the work quickly.
slow: My car is slow.	slowly: I drove slowly to the store.

There are some spelling changes, for example final –e (when it follows more than one consonant: terrible) is dropped. If it only follows one consonant –e (complete), e isn't dropped.

ADJECTIVE	ADVERB
terrible: The report is terrible.	terribly: They wrote the report terribly.
possible: Snow is possible tomorrow.	possibly: It will possibly snow tomorrow.
complete: Her book is complete.	completely: She completely finished her book.
rare: Rain is rare in the desert.	rarely: It rarely rains in the desert.

If an adjective ends in –y, the adverbial form ends in –ily. If an adjective ends in –ful, the adverb ends in –fully.

ADJECTIVE	ADVERB
hungry: Jack is hungry and wants to eat.	hungrily: Jack ate his dinner hungrily.
happy: Jill is a happy student.	happily: Jill studies happily.
beautiful: Gloria is a beautiful dancer.	beautifully: Gloria dances beautifully.
careful: I am a careful driver.	carefully: I drive carefully.

The adjective **good** has the adverbial form **well**. You are **good** at something, but you do something **well**. Additionally, while the adjective **bad** has the adverbial form **badly**, it is also common to use the adverbial form of **poor**, **poorly**, instead.

ADJECTIVE	ADVERB
good: John's Spanish is good.	well: John speaks Spanish well.
bad: John is a bad singer.	badly, poorly: John sings badly. John sings poorly.

Not all adverbs end in –ly. Here are some common ones.

Jack is very happy at his new university.	
It's twelve thirty; Karen just left for lunch two minutes ago.	
It's Friday, so we have the day off from work tomorrow.	
There is very little water in my glass; it's almost empty.	
In January, it's too cold for swimming!	
Maybe John is at work, but it's early, so maybe he's still at home.	
It's nine-thirty, so Noreen is at work now.	

Many common adverbs are adverbs of time or frequency. They tell you how often something is done. **Always** means all the time, and **never** means none of the time. Here are common adverbs of time, in order from **always** to **never**.

always: Jose always speaks Spanish with his family.	
usually: I usually have lunch at twelve thirty.	

The Simple Past Tense

Adverbs and Adverbial
Phrases with –ing

Prepositions of Time and
Other Useful Prepositions

Infinitives of Purpose

frequently: We frequently go to that restaurant.	
generally: Mary generally works five days a week.	
often: I often see my neighbors in the morning before work.	
sometimes: Sometimes I walk to work if the weather is nice.	
occasionally: Occasionally we have to stay late and finish our work.	
seldom: Mary is healthy, and seldom stays home sick.	
rarely: Jack rarely stays up past midnight, because he gets up very early for work.	
hardly ever: It hardly ever rains in the desert.	
never: I never take the bus to work; I drive or take the train.	

If you use before, after, or while with the –ing form of a verb, you have an adverbial phrase that expresses when something happens in relation to another action.

We left class at noon. We had lunch at twelve-thirty. After leaving class, we had lunch.	

Here are some other examples:

After getting home, Bob sat down and had dinner.	

I love to read in bed before falling asleep.	
Sue always gets nervous while giving a presentation.	

✎ Work Out 1

Complete each sentence with an adverb or –ing adverbial phrase, following the example.

Example: Warren drives _____ to work. (slow)
Answer: **Warren drives slowly to work.**

1. We_____ eat dinner around seven thirty. (general)

2. _____ it didn't rain during the football game. (lucky)

3. She_____ didn't get home until after six o'clock. (probable)

4. Brian_____ closed the door and went to bed. (quiet)

5. Elena really sings very_____. (good)

6. Frank_____ stood and began to give his presentation.

   (nervous)

7. After_____ to work, I always drink a cup of coffee. (get)

8. We set the table before_____ dinner. (eat)

9. Nick does the dishes very_____. (bad)

10. The students cannot speak while_____ an exam. (take)

ANSWER KEY
1. generally; 2. Luckily; 3. probably; 4. quietly; 5. well; 6. nervously; 7. getting; 8. eating; 9. badly /
poorly; 10. taking

The Simple Past Tense

Adverbs and Adverbial
Phrases with –ing

Prepositions of Time and
Other Useful Prepositions

Infinitives of Purpose

Phrase Builder 2

▶ 6C Phrase Builder 2 (CD 5, Track 4)

to enroll in school	
to take a class	
to sign up for a class	
to study for a test/an exam	
to do well on a test/an exam	
to pass a test/an exam	
to fail a test/an exam	
to do homework	
to do research	
to look up an answer	
to get good grades	
to get bad grades	
to graduate from high school	
to get a bachelor's degree	
to get a master's degree	
to write a dissertation	
to get a PhD/a doctorate	

✎ Word Practice 2

Fill in the blank with the best word from Phrase Builder 2.

1. To_____ in school means to start going to school.

2. Aaron wants to learn Chinese, so he's_____ up for a Chinese class.

3. Julie can't go to the party tonight because she has to_____ for a test.

4. I_____ the exam! I did really well on it.

5. I didn't pass my exam. I_____.

6. Many students do_____ online, not just at the library.

7. If you don't know the answer, you can_____ it up in your textbook.

8. Martha is a very good student. She gets good_____ in school.

9. Sam is_____ from high school this June. He's going to

    college next year.

10. After four years of college, you'll get a_____ degree.

11. Wendy is in graduate school, but she doesn't want a PhD. She wants

    a_____ degree.

12. If you want a PhD, you have to write a_____.

ANSWER KEY
1. **enroll**; 2. **signing**; 3. **study**; 4. **passed**; 5. **failed**; 6. **research**; 7. **look**; 8. **grades**; 9. **graduating**; 10.
bachelor's; 11. **master's**; 12. **dissertation**

Grammar Builder 2
▶ 6D Grammar Builder 2 (CD 5, Track 5)

INFINITIVES OF PURPOSE

The infinitive is the **to** form of a verb: **to do, to go, to make**. In Lesson 9 of
Essential English, you learned that you use the infinitive with **want, have**, and
need.

I want <u>to buy</u> a new computer, but I don't have enough money.	
Jack has <u>to study</u> tonight; he has a test tomorrow.	

The Simple Past Tense

Adverbs and Adverbial
Phrases with –ing

Prepositions of Time and
Other Useful Prepositions

Infinitives of Purpose

The flight leaves in an hour! We really need to get to the airport!	

The infinitive has many uses in English, and we'll look at them later in this course. For now, let's look at the "infinitive of purpose," which expresses a purpose or a reason.

We went to the post office to get stamps.	
Can you go to the supermarket to buy some milk and eggs?	
To buy something online, you need a credit card.	
We need flour, sugar, and eggs to bake a cake.	

You can also use in order in front of the infinitive: in order to pass, in order to make. This is a little more formal, but it means the same thing as to pass or to make.

In order to pass this class, you have to study much harder.	
You need your high school transcript in order to enroll in a college or university.	

Work Out 2

Answer the questions with an infinitive of purpose, following the example.

Example: What do you need to do in order to get a PhD? (write a dissertation)
Answer: In order to get a PhD, you need to write a dissertation.

1. What do you need to have in order to drive a car? (**a driver's license**)

   _____

2. Who do you need to speak with to get a raise? (**your boss**)

   _____

3. What do you need to do to pass the exam? (**study hard**)

   _____

4. Where is John going to get gas? (**the gas station**)

   _____

5. What did Sue buy to learn Japanese? (**a Japanese course**)

   _____

6. Why are they going to the store? (**buy a new computer**)

   _____

7. Why is Paul going to the post office? (**get stamps**)

   _____

8. What should you do in order to get into a good college? (**get good grades**)

   _____

ANSWER KEY
1. In order to drive a car, you need to have a driver's license. 2. You need to speak with your boss
to get a raise. 3. You need to study hard to pass the exam. 4. John is going to the gas station to get
gas. 5. Sue bought a Japanese course to learn Japanese. 6. They're going to the store to buy a new
computer. 7. Paul is going to the post office to get stamps. 8. You should get good grades in order to
get into a good college.

The Simple Past Tense

Adverbs and Adverbial
Phrases with –ing

Prepositions of Time and
Other Useful Prepositions

Infinitives of Purpose

✎ Drive It Home

Complete the sentence with either an –ing form of the verb in parentheses or its infinitive.

1. Before_____ this class, you need to enroll. (take)

2. I listen to podcasts while_____ the bus to work. (take)

3. After_____ the exam, I felt good. (take)

4. Don't talk while_____ the exam. (take)

5. We worked for four hours before_____ a break. (take)

6. We are going to the supermarket_____ some fruit. (get)

7. I want_____ some stamps; we have to go to the post office. (get)

8. You need_____ a new computer. (get)

9. Sue has to take the bus_____ to work. (get)

10. You should get good grades in order_____ into college. (get)

ANSWER KEY
1-5 all **taking**; 6-10 all **to get**

How Did You Do?

Let's see how you did in this lesson. By now, you should be able to:

☐ use adverbs and adverbial phrases with –ing
(Still unsure? Jump back to page 105.)

☐ use infinitives to express purpose (**to go, in order to go**)
(Still unsure? Jump back to page 111.)

✎ Word Recall

Match the infinitive in the left column with the place in the right column where that action takes place.

1. to commute to work	a. grocery store
2. to work late	b. office
3. to buy milk and eggs	c. conference room
4. to get stamps	d. gas station
5. to bake a cake	e. school
6. to give a presentation	f. bus
7. to get gas	g. post office
8. to study	h. kitchen

ANSWER KEY
1. f; 2. b; 3. a; 4. g; 5. h; 6. c; 7. d; 8. e

Lesson 7: Sentences

In this lesson you'll learn how to:

☐ talk about the future using different tenses (**I'll take, I'll be taking, I'm taking**)

☐ use coordinating conjunctions such as **and**, **but**, and **or**

Sentence Builder 1

▶ 7A Sentence Builder 1 (CD 5, Track 6)

Are you signing up for classes next semester?	
Are you going to sign up for Japanese 101?	

The Simple Past Tense

Adverbs and Adverbial
Phrases with –ing

Prepositions of Time and
Other Useful Prepositions

Infinitives of Purpose

I'm taking management classes this summer.	
We will take European History in the fall.	
She is going to go to school.	
Are you going to be in the office tomorrow?	
I'll be there early to write a report.	
I'll stay late at work tonight to finish it.	
Bill will be coming in late to work.	
The commute to work by train will be bad because of construction next week.	
Bill will be late to work.	
Sarah is going to be late to work.	
We are taking the day off tomorrow.	
He is interviewing for the job next week.	
When will he be interviewing?	
He's going to have his interview on Monday.	
He is giving his presentation on Tuesday.	

✎ Sentence Practice 1

Listen to the Sentence Builder again and fill in the words that are missing.

1. _____ for classes next semester?

2. Are you_____ sign up for Japanese 101?

3. I'm_____ management classes this summer.

4. We_____ European History in the fall.

5. She_____ go to school.

6. Are you_____ in the office tomorrow?

7. _____ there early to write a report.

8. _____ at work tonight to finish it.

9. Bill_____ in late to work.

10. The commute to work by train_____ because of
    construction next week.

11. Bill_____ late to work.

12. Sarah_____ late to work.

13. We_____ the day off tomorrow.

14. He_____ for the job next week.

15. When will he_____?

16. He's_____ his interview on Monday.

17. He_____ his presentation on Tuesday.

ANSWER KEY

1. Are you signing up; 2. going to; 3. taking; 4. will take; 5. is going to; 6. going to be; 7. I'll be; 8.
I'll stay late; 9. will be coming; 10. will be bad; 11. will be; 12. is going to be; 13. are taking; 14. is
interviewing; 15. be interviewing; 16. going to have; 17. is giving

The Simple Past Tense

Adverbs and Adverbial
Phrases with –ing

Prepositions of Time and
Other Useful Prepositions

Infinitives of Purpose

Grammar Builder 1

⊙ 7B Grammar Builder 1 (CD 5, Track 7)

EXPRESSING THE FUTURE

To talk about something in the future, you can use **will** + verb.

I will finish the report on Monday.	
Bill will be two hours late to work today.	

In negative statements, the negative comes between **will** and the verb. **Will** and **not** contract to form **won't**.

I will not finish the report on Monday.	
I won't finish the report on Monday.	

In questions, **will** comes before the pronoun.

Will you come into the office this weekend?	
Will we finish the report in time?	

You can also use **to be going to** + verb.

We are going to do our homework after dinner.	
A new school is going to be built next year.	
Bill and Andrea are going to pass the test.	

In questions, the pronoun and **to be** are inverted.

Are we going to do our homework after dinner?	
Is a new school going to be built next year?	

In negatives statements, the negative comes between **to be** and going. Remember the contraction with **to be**.

We are not going to do our homework after dinner.	
A new school isn't going to be built next year.	

You can also talk about the future using the present progressive + a future time expression.

They are enrolling in school next semester.	
We are working on the Simpson project next month.	
James is interviewing a new assistant at 3 o'clock.	

All of these future expressions mean the same thing.

I will interview Dave next Monday.	
I am going to interview Dave next Monday.	
I am interviewing Dave next Monday.	

The Simple Past Tense

Adverbs and Adverbial
Phrases with –ing

Prepositions of Time and
Other Useful Prepositions

Infinitives of Purpose

With the verb to be, the present progressive is not often used to express the future. Use either will + be or to be going to + be instead.

They will be in the office on Saturday.	
They are going to be in the office on Saturday.	

✎ Work Out 1

Rewrite each sentence in the future tense three different ways (or two, in the case of to be).

Example: I buy apples. (tomorrow)
Answer: I will buy apples tomorrow. I am going to buy apples tomorrow. I am buying apples tomorrow.

1. I write the report. (this afternoon)

   _____

2. We take our kids to school. (tomorrow morning)

   _____

3. They study Japanese. (next year)

   _____

4. The report is finished. (next week)

   _____

5. You come with us? (tonight)

_____

6. He doesn't work late. (on Wednesday)

_____

7. We don't go to work. (this Thursday)

_____

8. John and Dave speak to their boss about a raise. (Monday morning)

_____

9. The train is late. (today)

_____

10. She sends the report over email. (in an hour)

_____

ANSWER KEY

1. I will write the report this afternoon. I am going to write the report this afternoon. I am writing the report this afternoon. 2. We will take our kids to school tomorrow morning. We are going to take our kids to school tomorrow morning. We are taking our kids to school tomorrow morning. 3. They will study Japanese next year. They are going to study Japanese next year. They are studying Japanese next year. 4. The report will be finished next week. The report is going to be finished next week. The report is being finished next week. 5. Will you come with us? Are you going to come with us? Are you coming with us? 6. He won't work late tonight. He isn't going to work late tonight. He isn't working late tonight. 7. We won't go to work this Thursday. We aren't going to go to work this Thursday. We aren't working this Thursday. 8. John and Dave will speak to their boss about a raise Monday morning. John and Dave are going to speak to their boss about a raise Monday morning. John and Dave are speaking to their boss about a raise Monday morning. 9. The train will be late today. The train is going to be late today. 10. She will send the report over email in an hour. She is going to send the report over email in an hour. She is sending the report over email in an hour.

The Simple Past Tense

Adverbs and Adverbial
Phrases with –ing

Prepositions of Time and
Other Useful Prepositions

Infinitives of Purpose

Sentence Builder 2

▶ 7C Sentence Builder 2 (CD 5, Track 8)

I'm going to work and getting started on the project early.	
He had to read the report and write a summary.	
You're enrolled in two classes, and you still have time for a full-time job?	
He will be at work today, but he'll be out next Tuesday.	
She told us she was going to study, but I think she was going out with friends, and that's not okay.	
She told me that wasn't necessary, but I did it anyway.	
I explained the situation, but she wasn't happy.	
Did they fire you, or did they let you stay?	
You were president of the company, and you were also the treasurer?	
Were you the president of the company, or were you the treasurer?	
She was the president of the company, but she was also the treasurer.	

✎ Sentence Practice 2

Listen to the audio again and fill in the missing words you hear.

1. I'm going to work and_____ on the project

   early.

2. He had to_____ and write a summary.

3. You're enrolled in two classes, and you still have time for_____

   _____?

4. He will be in work today, but_____ next Tuesday.

5. She told us she was going to study,_____ I think she was going out with

   friends, _____ that's not okay.

6. She told me that wasn't necessary, but_____.

7. I explained the situation,_____ she wasn't happy.

8. Did they fire you,_____ did they let you stay?

9. You were_____ of the company, _____you were also

   the treasurer?

10. Were you the president of the_____, _____ were you

    the treasurer?

11. She was the president of the company,_____ she was also the

    _____.

ANSWER KEY

1. getting started; 2. read the report; 3. a full-time job; 4. he'll be out; 5. but, and; 6. I did it anyway;
7. but; 8. or; 9. president, and; 10. company, or; 11. but, treasurer

The Simple Past Tense

Adverbs and Adverbial
Phrases with –ing

Prepositions of Time and
Other Useful Prepositions

Infinitives of Purpose

Grammar Builder 2

▶ 7D Grammar Builder 2 (CD 5, Track 9)

COORDINATING CONJUNCTIONS

Coordinating conjunctions are words like **and, but,** and **or** that bring two sentences together to form one sentence. The sentence on either side of the conjunction can stand on its own.

I'm going to work early. I'm finishing work on my presentation. I'm going to work early, <u>and</u> (I'm) finishing work on my presentation.	
He's interviewing Dave on Tuesday. He already decided who to hire. He's interviewing Dave on Tuesday, <u>but</u> he already decided who to hire.	
We have to finish this project. We'll be in trouble. We have to finish this project, <u>or</u> we'll be in trouble.	

Notice that the sentences are often separated by a comma (,). Also note that it's sometimes possible to omit the pronoun from the fragment that follows the conjunction **and**.

And introduces a sentence that adds information to the previous sentence. **But** and **yet** introduce a sentence that contradicts information in the previous sentence. **Or** introduces a sentence that offers an alternative to the previous sentence.

We are going to work, and we are going to finish the project.	

Coordinating Conjunctions   Relative Clauses:
                                             that, who/whom, which

We are going to work, but/yet we are not going to finish the project.	
Are we going to finish the project, or are we not going to finish the project?	

Other coordinating conjunctions are for, nor, and so. For introduces a reason, nor introduces a negative statement, so introduces a consequence of the first clause.

We are not going to finish the project, for we are not going to work.	
We are not going to work, nor are we going to finish the project.	
We did not go to work, so we did not finish the project.	

Notice that when using nor, the verb and the subject are switched in the following clause.

Work Out 2

Combine the two sentences using the coordinating conjunction given in parentheses.

1. He is going to work. He is going to finish his sales summary. (and)

   _____

2. The marketing department finished their project. They didn't finish it in time for the meeting. (but)

   _____

The Simple Past Tense

Adverbs and Adverbial
Phrases with –ing

Prepositions of Time and
Other Useful Prepositions

Infinitives of Purpose

3. He didn't finish his project. He did show up for work today. (**nor**)

_____

4. Are you coming to dinner? Are you going to stay late at work? (**or**)

_____

5. He will be getting to work late today. The trains were running late. (**for**)

_____

6. We got to school early. We were able to study before the test. (**so**)

_____

7. She gave me a present. She told me I was doing a good job. (**and**)

_____

8. There is enough time to finish our work. We don't have the energy to do it. (**yet**)

_____

9. Will you be eating dinner alone tonight? Will you be coming with us? (**or**)

_____

10. She said that she was going out with friends. She stayed home instead. (**but**)

_____

ANSWER KEY
1. He is going to work and (he is going to) finish his sales summary. 2. The marketing department finished their project, but they didn't finish it in time for the meeting. 3. He didn't finish his project, nor did he show up for work today. 4. Are you coming to dinner, or are you going to stay late at work? 5. He will be getting to work late today, for the trains were running late. 6. We got to school early, so we were able to study before the test. 7. She gave me a present, and (she) told me I was doing a good job. 8. There is enough time to finish our work, yet we don't have the energy to do it. 9. Will you be eating dinner alone tonight or will you be coming with us? 10. She said that she was going out with friends, but she stayed home instead.

Intermediate English

✎ Drive It Home

Complete the following sentences in the future tense.

1. We_____ be going to work early today.

2. They_____ go to school next week.

3. She_____ be seeing Tom on Friday.

4. _____ you come to dinner on Sunday?

5. I_____ not be late to work again.

6. When are you_____ be getting into the city?

7. If I come into work early, is he_____ help me with the project?

8. Sales and marketing are_____ be merging into one department.

9. Only the smartest person is_____ know the answer.

10. The report is_____ be finished in the morning.

ANSWER KEY
1-5 all will; 6-10 all going to

How Did You Do?

Let's see how you did in this lesson. By now, you should be able to:

☐ talk about the future using different tenses (**I'll take, I'll be taking, I'm taking**)
(Still unsure? Jump back to page 118.)

☐ use coordinating conjunctions such as **and**, **but**, and **or**
(Still unsure? Jump back to page 124.)

The Simple Past Tense

Adverbs and Adverbial
Phrases with –ing

Prepositions of Time and
Other Useful Prepositions

Infinitives of Purpose

✎ Word Recall

Let's review coordinating conjunctions. Pick the best conjunction to complete the sentence.

1. Every Saturday morning we get up early, (**but**/**or**) this Saturday we're sleeping in.

2. They're leaving the house at seven (**but**/**and**) they're catching a nine thirty flight tomorrow.

3. Sonia is studying tonight, (**for**/**or**) she's taking a test tomorrow.

4. Tomorrow night we're eating dinner at a restaurant (**nor**/**and**) on Saturday night we'll be watching a movie.

5. On Monday through Thursday Jill leaves work early (**yet**/**for**) on Fridays she leaves work late.

6. Bill doesn't like orange juice, (**nor**/**so**) does he like pancakes for breakfast.

7. This week John is home sick, (**yet**/**so**) he's sleeping late every morning.

8. Are we going to the movies, (**or**/**yet**) are we staying in?

ANSWER KEY
1. but; 2. and; 3. for; 4. and; 5. yet; 6. nor; 7. so; 8. or

Lesson 8: Conversations

By the end of this lesson, you should be able to:

☐ use subordinating conjunctions such as **because, when, as soon as,** etc.

☐ use relative clauses **that, who/whom,** and **which** to offer more information in a
sentence

⒬ Conversation 1
▶ 8A Conversation 1 (CD 5, Track 10)

*Bill started a new job today. He's meeting one of friends for dinner. Listen in as he
talks about his day.*

Mike:	So, how was the first day of the new job that you got?
Bill:	Don't ask!
Mike:	Oh, come on. It can't be that bad.
Bill:	Really? It can't? I overslept and missed my train.
Mike:	Oh, ouch. Late on the first day? That's not good.
Bill:	No, it's not. And after I waited for the next train, which was five minutes late, I got on and saw that there weren't any free seats. So I had to stand for the whole time that it took to get into the city.
Mike:	So, you stood for your commute. That's not so terrible. It'll probably happen again. These things happen when you commute. How late were you to work?
Bill:	Forty minutes. And I couldn't even call in because my cell phone battery died!
Mike:	Oh, no. This story keeps getting worse! What did you say when you got into the office?
Bill:	What could I say? I apologized and explained, but my boss obviously wasn't happy. I said, "I'll stay late tonight and make up the time." She told me that wasn't necessary, but I understood that I'm going to have to work very hard and hope that she'll forgive me.
Mike:	She'll see that you're not irresponsible. This was just one mistake.

The Simple Past Tense

Adverbs and Adverbial
Phrases with –ing

Prepositions of Time and
Other Useful Prepositions

Infinitives of Purpose

Bill:	No, it wasn't just one mistake.
Mike:	Uh oh. There were other mistakes?
Bill:	Yes. I walked to my desk, sat down, and started to work. I had to read a couple of reports and write a summary.
Mike:	So? That doesn't sound bad.
Bill:	It wasn't. I was so focused on it that I didn't pay attention to the time.
Mike:	Oh, no . . .
Bill:	Yup. So I was fifteen minutes late to the first meeting that I had. The woman who sits next to me ran back from the meeting room and said, "Bill, everyone's waiting for you!"
Mike:	That's awful. What did your boss say?
Bill:	She said, "Bill, I'd like to see you in my office after this meeting."
Mike:	Not good. Did she fire you?
Bill:	No, she gave me a gift.
Mike:	A gift? You were late twice on your first day of work, and you got a gift?
Bill:	Yup, a beautiful, handy, brand new . . . watch.
Mike:	Well, at least your boss thought of something that you really need!

✎ Conversation Practice 1

Answer the questions below based on the conversation. If you need to go back and listen again, feel free to do so.

1. Why did Bill miss his train?

2. Why did Bill have to stand for the whole time on the train?

3. How late was Bill to work?

_____

4. What did Bill say to his boss when he got to work?

_____

5. What did Bill do when he got to his desk?

_____

6. Why was Bill late to his first meeting?

_____

7. Who told Bill he was late to the meeting?

_____

8. What did Bill's boss give him because he was late?

_____

ANSWER KEY

1. He overslept. 2. He had to stand because there weren't any free seats. 3. Bill was forty minutes late. 4. He said, "I'll stay late and make up the time." 5. He read a couple of reports and wrote a summary. 6. He was late because he was so focused on his work that he didn't pay attention to the time. 7. The woman who sits next to him told him he was late. 8. She gave him a beautiful, handy, brand new watch.

Grammar Builder 1
▶ 8B Grammar Builder 1 (CD 5, Track 11)

SUBORDINATING CONJUNCTIONS

Subordinating conjunctions are words that connect a subordinate clause with a main clause. Some examples of subordinating conjunctions are after, before, when, while, because, since, as, as soon as, unless, if, even though. The

The Simple Past Tense

Adverbs and Adverbial
Phrases with –ing

Prepositions of Time and
Other Useful Prepositions

Infinitives of Purpose

subordinate clause derives its meaning from the main clause. Often, subordinating conjunctions can also be prepositions.

<u>After</u> you enroll, you can take this class.	
<u>Before</u> you can take this class, you have to enroll.	
<u>When</u> you enroll, you can take this class.	
You can't take this class <u>while</u> you're not enrolled.	
You can't take this class <u>because</u> you're not enrolled.	
You can't take this class <u>since</u> you're not enrolled.	
You can't take this class, <u>as</u> you need to enroll.	
You can take this class, <u>as soon as</u> you enroll.	
<u>Unless</u> you enroll in this class, you can't take it.	
<u>If</u> you want to take this class, you have to enroll.	
<u>Even though</u> you enrolled, you still can't take this class (because it's full).	

Notice that there are small changes in meaning, but in each example, the conjunction comes before the subordinate clause. Also note that the subordinate (or dependent) clause cannot exist on its own; this is called a **sentence fragment**. So, for example, you won't see the sentence **Even though she applied for the job.** in everyday English, although you may see it in some colloquial instances.

Intermediate English

Take It Further
SUBORDINATING CONJUNCTIONS WITH AS

Many subordinating conjunctions contain the word as. Let's look at a few of them.

as He is getting a promotion, as he is the best employee.	
as long as He will get a promotion, as long as he keeps up the good work.	
as soon as He will get a raise, as soon as he gets a promotion.	
as far as He is getting a promotion, as far as the boss is concerned.	
as if He is acting confident, as if he already got a promotion.	
as though He is acting as though he already got a promotion.	

Notice that the subordinate conjunction as far as is used most often in the expression as far as (someone/something) is concerned.

As far as I'm concerned, you're the best person for the job.	

The Simple Past Tense

Adverbs and Adverbial
Phrases with –ing

Prepositions of Time and
Other Useful Prepositions

Infinitives of Purpose

As far as the project is concerned, we're confident we can finish it on time.	

✎ Work Out 1

Choose the subordinating conjunction that best completes each sentence.

1. _____ we got a full-time job, we had no time for vacation.

   a. Before

   b. After

   c. As far as

   d. As though

2. He will start the meeting_____ the sales department gets here.

   a. as though

   b. before

   c. even though

   d. when

3. She is acting_____ she is the president of the company.

   a. as if

   b. because

   c. unless

   d. while

4. We need medical benefits ________ we have to go to the doctor.

a. **unless**

b. **because**

c. **while**

d. **after**

5. ________ her assistant told her she was late for the meeting, she ended the phone call.

a. **Unless**

b. **As far as**

c. **When**

d. **As though**

6. ________ you are taking a vacation, you need to be at work.

a. **As long as**

b. **Unless**

c. **While**

d. **As**

7. ________ you get here, we will start the meeting.

a. **As long as**

b. **As soon as**

c. **As though**

d. **As if**

The Simple Past Tense

Adverbs and Adverbial
Phrases with –ing

Prepositions of Time and
Other Useful Prepositions

Infinitives of Purpose

8. _____ you want a raise, you need to work harder.

   a. **As far as**

   b. **As though**

   c. **While**

   d. **If**

9. **They are studying**_____ **they wait for the bus.**

   a. **while**

   b. **because**

   c. **as soon as**

   d. **as far as**

10. **John will apply for the job**_____ **he isn't qualified.**

    a. **while**

    b. **even though**

    c. **when**

    d. **as soon as**

    ANSWER KEY
    1. b; 2. d; 3. a; 4. b; 5. c; 6. b; 7. b; 8. d; 9. a; 10. b

ᴄᴄ Conversation 2
▶ 8C Conversation 2 (CD 5, Track 12)

Elizabeth and Kim are roommates in their first year at a university. It's the beginning of the semester, and they're discussing their new classes. Listen in.

Kim:	So, which classes are you taking?
Elizabeth:	I'm not completely sure yet. I signed up for Japanese 101, Early Twentieth-Century European History, Intro to English Literature, Biology 101, and Intro to Digital Communications.
Kim:	Intro to Digital Communications? What's that?
Elizabeth:	You know, the Internet, social media, that sort of thing.
Kim:	Well, you'll be good at that! You get on the Internet as soon as you get back to the dorm room! And you text me more often than you talk to me!
Elizabeth:	Very funny. But I'm not so sure about Japanese 101.
Kim:	Why not? This morning you were excited about the class and said that you really want to learn Japanese.
Elizabeth:	I do want to learn Japanese, but after I got to the class, I wasn't so sure.
Kim:	Why not?
Elizabeth:	As soon as the professor got into the room, she started speaking Japanese.
Kim:	Well, did you want her to speak Portuguese?
Elizabeth:	Ha ha. No, I mean she only spoke Japanese during the whole class. It's a beginner's class, so I didn't expect only Japanese.
Kim:	Well, that's normal in language classes. You'll start to understand her gradually.
Elizabeth:	Yeah, but the other students speak a little already, and I don't know anything. The guy who sits in front of me had a whole conversation in Japanese with the professor!
Kim:	Come on, you're exaggerating. You said you took Japanese in high school.
Elizabeth:	Yes, but I only took one year. But this guy, he said his name, and he told the professor the name of the town where he lives, and he said that this is his second year at the university.

The Simple Past Tense

Adverbs and Adverbial
Phrases with –ing

Prepositions of Time and
Other Useful Prepositions

Infinitives of Purpose

Kim:	He did all of that in Japanese?
Elizabeth:	Yeah! I couldn't believe it!
Kim:	Elizabeth, don't you see? You listened to him as he said all of that, and you understood him even though he spoke in Japanese.
Elizabeth:	I understood, but when the professor talked to me, I could only say "Hello. My name is Elizabeth."
Kim:	Well, that's a start!
Elizabeth:	I think it's going to be a very hard class.
Kim:	Well, you're taking the class so that you can learn to speak. You'll learn. Just be patient. Now, let's go to a restaurant to celebrate the first day of classes.
Elizabeth:	Alright. I am hungry. What do you feel like eating?
Kim:	Hmmm . . . I think I'd like to have some sushi. You can order for us!
Elizabeth:	Very funny.

✎ Conversation Practice 2

Answer the questions based on the conversation. If you're unsure of the answer, listen to the conversation on your audio one more time.

1. What classes has Elizabeth signed up for?

_____

2. What do they study in Intro to Digital Communications?

_____

3. Why is Elizabeth not sure about Japanese 101?

_____

4. What did the guy who sits in front of Elizabeth do?

_____

5. Did Elizabeth study Japanese in high school?

_____

6. What did the guy say to the professor in Japanese?

_____

7. What did Elizabeth say to the professor in Japanese?

_____

8. Where are Kim and Elizabeth going to celebrate the first day of classes?

_____

ANSWER KEY
1. She's signed up for Japanese 101, Early Twentieth-Century European History, Intro to English Literature, Biology 101, and Intro to Digital Communications 2. They study the Internet and social media. 3. She is unsure because the professor only speaks Japanese in class. 4. He had a whole conversation in Japanese with the professor. 5. Yes, she took one year. 6. He said his name, told the professor the name of the town where he lives, and said that this is his second year at the university. 7. She said, "Hello. My name is Elizabeth." 8. They are going to a restaurant to eat sushi.

Grammar Builder 2
▶ 8D Grammar Builder 2 (CD 5, Track 13)

RELATIVE CLAUSES: THAT, WHO/WHOM, WHICH

You have already seen the words who/whom and which used as questions, and the word that used as a demonstrative pronoun.

Which classes are you taking?	
Who is teaching the class this year?	
That class is a good class.	

The Simple Past Tense

Adverbs and Adverbial
Phrases with –ing

Prepositions of Time and
Other Useful Prepositions

Infinitives of Purpose

These words can also be used to introduce relative clauses. Relative clauses are clauses introduced by the words **that**, **who/whom**, and **which**. The clauses following these words act as adjective phrases, modifying the preceding sentence, and giving new information about the subject or object.

In relative clauses, **which** is used for things, while **who** is used for people. **That** can be used with both people and things.

The teacher is Japanese. She teaches this class. The teacher who/that teaches this class is Japanese.	
This is the Japanese class. It is required to graduate. This is the Japanese class which/that is required to graduate.	

The only difference when the relative clauses are used for the object is that **whom** is used instead of **who** in more formal English.

The teacher is Japanese. I had her today in class. The teacher who(m)/that I had today in class is Japanese.	
This is the Japanese class. We took this class last year. This is the Japanese class which/that we took last year.	

When the relative clause is used as the object of a verb, that/which/who(m) is often omitted.

The teacher I had today in class is Japanese.	
This is the Japanese class we took last year.	

You can punctuate the relative clauses with commas only when the clause is unnecessary. Additionally, you cannot use that when the relative clause is unnecessary; use who(m) or which instead.

Mr. Blake, who studied Japanese for four years in Nagasaki, is teaching this class.	
The class, which will teach beginner level Japanese, starts on Monday.	

✎ Work Out 2

Circle the correct word to complete each sentence.

1. The history class (who/that) I signed up for starts this Monday.

2. The guy (who/whom) sits next to me in class knows a lot of Japanese.

3. The teacher (who/whom) teaches the class is Portuguese.

4. I am bringing the book (who/that) you let me borrow last week.

5. Is this the guy (which/that) you were talking about?

6. The express bus, (which/that) arrives every ten minutes, is late.

7. I saw the girl (who/which) you were telling me about.

The Simple Past Tense

Adverbs and Adverbial
Phrases with –ing

Prepositions of Time and
Other Useful Prepositions

Infinitives of Purpose

8. Ms. Anderson, (whom/that) I have known since childhood, is coming to visit on Sunday.

9. We should go to the restaurant (who/that) has sushi.

10. I saw the film (who/that) you recommended to me last night.

ANSWER KEY
1. that; 2. who; 3. who; 4. that; 5. that; 6. which; 7. who; 8. whom; 9. that; 10. that

✎ Drive It Home

Complete the following sentences with **that**.

1. I saw the film_____ you recommended.

2. The teacher_____ is teaching this class is very smart.

3. Will we see the work_____ you have done?

4. We know the girl_____ you are dating.

5. We're meeting the guy_____ will be in our study group.

6. This is the school_____ has the best Japanese courses.

7. I like movies_____ are about dance.

8. The pencil_____ is in my bag needs to be sharpened.

9. We gave the professor_____ taught our class a gift at the end of the year.

10. The gift_____we gave her was expensive.

ANSWER KEY
1-10 all **that**

⊕ Culture Note
THE AMERICAN WORK ETHIC

In America, there is the simple belief that if a person works hard enough, success can and will follow naturally. This notion has been a part of the American landscape since the country's birth. The promise of hard work and sacrifice in order to create a kind of heaven on earth captured the imagination of many people in the early history of this country, and this opportunity was in fact exactly what motivated so many to leave their homelands and settle in America. This ideal survives today, seen as the model for success in any area of life—in education, in any profession, in sports, or in any skill.

In the workplace, this ambitious work ethic often translates to the expectation for an employee to be involved in all projects at all times. Most American offices have a rigid timetable; you are expected to arrive to work on time and stay until the work day is over. People expecting to be promoted often work extra hours, sometimes without pay. Some people argue that this allows for more productivity; others might argue that longer work hours and less vacation actually make Americans less productive.

How Did You Do?

Let's see how you did in this lesson. By now, you should be able to:

☐ use subordinating conjunctions such as because, when, as soon as, etc. (Still unsure? Jump back to page 131.)

☐ use relative clauses that, who/whom, and which to offer more information in a sentence (Still unsure? Jump back to page 139.)

✎ Word Recall

Choose the best subordinating conjunction to complete each sentence.

after, before, when, while, because, since, as, as soon as, as long as, as far as, as though, as if, unless, if, even though

1. We are going to work by bus, (since/even though) a car would be faster.

2. (After/As) we go to the movie, we will go to a restaurant for dinner.

3. I was late for work (because/as soon as) the bus was late.

4. She goes to the gym in the morning (before/after) she goes to work.

5. (Unless/If) the bus is on time, we will be late to work.

6. I love to read at night, (until/as long as) I have the time.

7. He will start the presentation (as soon as/as long as) the marketing team arrives.

8. The class will begin on time (as/as far as) the professor is concerned.

ANSWER KEY
1. even though; 2. After; 3. because; 4. before; 5. Unless; 6. as long as; 7. as soon as; 8. as far as

Don't forget to practice and reinforce what you've learned by visiting **www.livinglanguage.com/ languagelab** for flashcards, games, and quizzes!

Unit 2 Quiz

Let's put the most essential English words and grammar points you've learned so far to practice in a few exercises. It's important to be sure that you've mastered this material before you move on. Score yourself at the end of the review and see if you need to go back for more practice, or if you're ready to move on to Unit 3.

A. Rewrite the sentences below in the simple past tense.

1. I work at a restaurant.

_____

2. He eats a lot of vegetables.

_____

3. She teaches English.

_____

4. They do yoga on their lunch break.

_____

B. Fill in the correct preposition.

1. I have physics class_____ Wednesday.

2. She went to bed_____ night.

3. What are we having_____ dinner?

C. Construct a sentence in the simple past tense from the words below. Be sure to transform the adjective into an adverb.

1. you, possible, be out when I called

_____

2. they, happy, take the job

_____

3. he, rare, go to the gym last year

_____

D. Answer the questions below using an infinitive of purpose.

1. Why did you go to the store? (get milk)

_____

2. Why did you need my credit card? (buy something online)

_____

3. Why do you need passing grades? (graduate)

_____

E. Rewrite the sentences below in the future tense.

1. We have friends over for dinner.

_____

2. Are you in town?

_____

3. I work this weekend.

_____

F. Connect the two sentences using before, but, or or. You will use each conjunction only once.

1. We have to finish this project. We will be fired.

   _____

2. You can take this class. You need to enroll.

   _____

3. She was in the office on Monday. She was not in the office on Tuesday.

   _____

G. Connect the two sentences using a relative clause.

1. She's the Japanese teacher. We had her last year.

   _____

2. This is the Japanese textbook. This textbook is required for class.

   _____

ANSWER KEY
A. 1. I worked at a restaurant. 2. He ate a lot of vegetables. 3. She taught English. 4. They did yoga on their lunch break.
B. 1. on; 2. at; 3. for
C. 1. You were possibly out when I called. 2. They happily took the job./They took the job happily. 3. He rarely went to the gym last year.
D. 1. I went to the store to get milk. 2. I needed your credit card to buy something online. 3. I need passing grades to graduate.
E. 1. We are having friends over for dinner./We will be having friends over for dinner./We are going to have friends over for dinner. 2. Will you be in town?/Are you going to be in town? 3. I am working this weekend./I will be working this weekend./I am going to be working this weekend.
F. 1. We have to finish this project or we will be fired. 2. Before you can take this class, you need to enroll. 3. She was in the office on Monday, but she was not in the office on Tuesday.
G. 1. She's the Japanese teacher who(m)/that we had last year. 2. This is the Japanese textbook which/that is required for class.

How Did You Do?

Give yourself a point for every correct answer, then use the following key to tell whether you're ready to move on:

0–7 points: It's probably a good idea to go back through the lesson again. You may be moving too quickly, or there may be too much "down time" between your contact with English. Remember that it's better to spend 30 minutes with English three or four times a week than it is to spend two or three hours just once a week. Find a pace that's comfortable for you, and spread your contact hours out as much as you can.

8–12 points: You would benefit from a review before moving on. Go back and spend a little more time on the specific points that gave you trouble. Re-read the Grammar Builder sections that were difficult, and do the work out one more time. Don't forget about the online supplemental practice material, either. Go to **www. livinglanguage.com/languagelab** for games and quizzes that will reinforce the material from this unit.

13–17 points: Good job! There are just a few points that you could consider reviewing before moving on. If you haven't worked with the games and quizzes on **www.livinglanguage.com/languagelab**, please give them a try.

18–20 points: Great! You're ready to move on to the next unit.

points

Unit 3:
Shopping and Running Errands

In this unit, you'll learn everything you need to feel comfortable going on a shopping trip. You'll learn vocabulary related to shopping at a grocery store and useful words for running errands. In this unit, you'll also expand on your grammar by learning the difference between the simple past and the present perfect tenses, how to say things like I have gone and I was going, and how to form and use tag questions. You'll also learn how to use quantifiers like both, each, every, and none and the usage of may and might.

Lesson 9: Words

In this lesson you'll learn:

☐ vocabulary related to shopping and parts of a grocery store

☐ the present perfect to say things like I have shopped

☐ vocabulary for setting up bank accounts and other money-related expressions

☐ irregular past participles such as gone, had, been

Word Builder 1

▶ 9A Word Builder 1 (CD 5, Track 14)

store, grocery store, thrift store, book store	

market, farmers market, flea market	
mall, shopping mall, strip mall	
bakery, deli, meat counter, dairy section, frozen food, snacks	
groceries, aisle, shelf, register, shopping list	
containers: carton, box, jar, basket, bag, bottle, can	
beverages: milk, juice, water, beer, wine, soft drinks, soda	
dairy: milk, sour cream, cheese, butter, eggs	
baking supplies: cereal, bread, flour, baking powder, baking soda, sugar, salt	
spices: pepper, cayenne, cumin, cinnamon	
herbs: basil, oregano, thyme, rosemary, sage, parsley	
sugar free, gluten free, fat free, low fat, low salt, diet, vegetarian	
to shop, to browse, to buy, to window shop, to bargain, to haggle, to compare	

✎ Word Practice 1

Answer the question or fill in the blank based on the vocabulary you learned in Word Builder 1.

1. You can find milk in the_____.

2. You can find chicken breasts at the_____.

3. Which of the following is not a spice: cumin, cinnamon, cereal,

    cayenne?_____

4. Foods that have no fat are called_____.

5. Food for people who don't eat meat is called_____.

6. When you go to the store, you make a_____ to

    remember what you need to buy.

7. When you are ready to pay, you take your groceries to the_____.

8. You can buy antiques at a_____.

9. Which of the following is not a beverage: juice, beer, sour cream,

    milk?_____

10. Flour, baking soda, sugar, and salt are_____.

ANSWER KEY

1. **dairy section**; 2. **meat counter**; 3. **cereal**; 4. **fat free**; 5. **vegetarian**; 6. **shopping list**; 7. **register**; 8. **flea market**; 9. **sour cream**; 10. **baking supplies**

Grammar Builder 1

▶ 9B Grammar Builder 1 (CD 5, Track 15)

THE PRESENT PERFECT TENSE

You learned one type of past tense, the simple past tense in Lesson 5. Let's now look at the present perfect tense. The present perfect tense is formed with the verb to have and the past participle of the main verb.

PRESENT PERFECT	
I have shopped	
you have shopped	
he/she has shopped	
we have shopped	
they have shopped	

The past participle in the above example is shopped. Most verbs will just use the past tense form of the verb as the past participle (worked, returned, finished). We'll look at irregular past participles in the next Grammar Builder.

The present perfect tense is used:

a) for an event that happened in the past when the exact time is not known
b) when there's a result or connection being made to the present
c) when the time period is still unfinished (so far this week, up to now, during my life)

We have listened to this record a hundred times.	
You have worked really hard this week.	
I have shopped here three times this month.	

In questions, the pronoun and has/have are inverted.

How long has she worked at this company?	

In negative statements, not comes between has/have and the verb.

I haven't worked this hard in years.	

Intermediate English

Take It Further
TIME EXPRESSIONS WITH PRESENT PERFECT TENSE

Since the present perfect tense is used only for unfinished time periods or when the exact time is unknown, you will see it with some specific time expressions. **Since**, **how long**, and **for** + a length of time are the most common expressions you will see with the present perfect tense.

since **I have wanted to be an astronaut since I was a little girl.**	
how long **How long have you lived in Chicago?**	
for + length of time **She has worked at this company for seven years.**	

Here are other time expressions used with the present perfect tense.

so far **So far I have watched three episodes of this show.**	
up to now **Up to now she has worked only for women.**	
during (habitual) **They have started watching television during dinner.**	
yet **We haven't talked to her yet about the party.**	

Note that **yet** is used most often with the present perfect tense in questions or negative statements.

✎ Work Out 1

Fill in the blank with the correct present perfect tense of the verb given in parentheses.

1. So far we_____ for seventeen hours this week. (**work**)

2. They_____ at that store before. (**shop**)

3. For how long_____ to be an actress? (**you, want**)

4. He_____ in Mississippi since he was a little boy. (**live**)

5. You_____ me seven times today. (**text**)

6. I_____ to call you three times. (**try**)

7. _____ the film yet? (**she, watch**)

8. We_____ to your message yet. (**listen, negative**)

9. They_____the chicken for dinner. (**cook, negative**)

10. I_____ the groceries from the store.

(**pick up, negative**)

ANSWER KEY
1. have worked; 2. have shopped; 3. have you wanted; 4. has lived; 5. have texted; 6. have tried; 7. Has she watched; 8. haven't listened; 9. haven't cooked; 10. haven't picked up

Word Builder 2

▶ 9C Word Builder 2 (CD 5, Track 16)

bank, branch, teller, window	
account, checking account, savings account, free checking, basic checking	
deposit, withdrawal, transfer, balance, debit, payment	
interest rate, investment, mortgage, online banking	
check, deposit slip, debit card, fees	
business, personal, minimum, maximum, overdrawn, competitive, automatic debit	
daily, weekly, monthly, annually	
to make a deposit, to deposit, to make a withdrawal, to withdraw, to transfer, to open an account, to close an account, to finance	

✎ Word Practice 2

Answer the question or fill in the blank based on the vocabulary you learned in Word Builder 2.

1. When you take money out of your bank account, you are making a

   _____.

2. An account that helps you save money is called a

   _____.

3. If you have a high_____ on your savings account,

   you will save more money.

4. Some banks make you pay_____ every month, the cost of keeping a

5. \bank account.

6. A payment you make every month is a_____ payment.

7. In order to use a bank's services, you first have to

   _____.

8. If you no longer want to use a bank's services, you will

   _____.

9. Some people prefer to use computers to do their banking, so they

   use_____.

10. We bought a house, and the bank financed our_____.

11. You can pay bills without doing anything by using

    _____.

ANSWER KEY
1. **withdrawal**; 2. **savings account**; 3. **interest rate**; 4. **fees**; 5. **monthly**; 6. **open an account**; 7. **close an account**; 8. **online banking**; 9. **mortgage**; 10. **automatic debit**

Grammar Builder 2
▶ 9D Grammar Builder 2 (CD 5, Track 17)

IRREGULAR PAST PARTICIPLES

By now you have learned the four principal parts of English verbs: the simple form, the simple past, the past participle, and the present participle (the –ing form). You saw in the previous Grammar Builder that the simple past and the past participle are often the same: **I shopped, I have shopped; she worked, she has** worked. Many verbs, however, have irregular past participles that are different from their simple past forms. Let's look at some of these irregular past participles now.

SIMPLE FORM	PAST PARTICIPLE
be	been
begin	begun
bring	brought
do	done
drink	drunk
drive	driven
eat	eaten
go	gone
get	gotten
have	had
know	known
see	seen
sing	sung
speak	spoken
take	taken
understand	understood
write	written

You can find more of these irregular past participles in the grammar summary.

Let's look at the use of some irregular past participles in sentences.

We have bought three bottles of wine for the party.	
Have you spoken to Bill about what we need to bring to lunch on Saturday?	

I haven't gotten the chicken breasts for dinner.	
She's driven to Chicago before.	

✎ Work Out 2

Fill in the blank with the correct past participle of the verb given in parentheses.

1. I have_____ three pages of this essay so far. (**write**)

2. They've_____ all the milk. (**drink**)

3. We've_____ too many bad experiences with banks before. (**have**)

4. She hasn't_____ her homework yet. (**do**)

5. He has_____ so many interesting people. (**know**)

6. Have they_____ to the grocery store yet? (**go**)

7. Have you_____ to Chicago before? (**be**)

8. We haven't_____to cook dinner yet. (**begin**)

9. She hasn't_____ the boys to swim practice. (**take**)

10. Have you_____ a word he's been saying? (**understand**)

ANSWER KEY
1. written; 2. drunk; 3. had; 4. done; 5. known; 6. gone; 7. been; 8. begun; 9. taken; 10. understood

✎ Drive It Home

Fill in the blank with the correct missing word.

1. I_____ deposited a check from work.

2. _____ you written the report yet?

3. We_____ opened a bank account at this branch.

4. They_____ watched this film seven times.

5. We would cook dinner, but we_____ done any shopping.

6. I_____ eaten all day.

7. You_____ worked this hard in years.

8. She_____ been to the store.

9. He_____ cooked a good meal tonight.

10. She_____ not seen this film.

ANSWER KEY
1-4 all have; 5-7 all haven't; 8-10 all has

How Did You Do?

Let's see how you did in this lesson. By now, you should be able to:

☐ talk about going shopping and name the parts of a grocery store (Still unsure? Jump back to page 149.)

☐ use the present perfect to say things like **I have shopped** (Still unsure? Jump back to page 151.)

☐ talk about opening a bank account and use other money-related expressions (Still unsure? Jump back to page 155.)

☐ use irregular past participles such as **gone, had, been** (Still unsure? Jump back to page 156.)

✎ Word Recall

Match the foods below with the section of the grocery store where you'd find them.

1. potato chips	a. meat section
2. chicken breasts	b. dairy
3. butter	c. baking supplies
4. cinnamon	d. frozen food
5. ice cream	e. bakery
6. soda	f. spices
7. flour	g. beverages
8. bread	h. snacks

ANSWER KEY
1. h; 2. a; 3. b; 4. f; 5. d; 6. g; 7. c; 8. e

Lesson 10: Phrases

In this lesson you'll learn:

☐ container nouns for food such as **carton of eggs** and **loaf of bread**

☐ the difference between the present perfect and the simple past

☐ expressions with the verb **make**

☐ how to use the past progressive (**I was going**)

Phrase Builder 1

▶ 10A Phrase Builder 1 (CD 5, Track 18)

loaf of bread	
slice of meat	
slice of cheese	
bunch of grapes	
bunch of lettuce	
a dozen eggs	
carton of eggs	
carton of milk	
carton of juice	
box of pasta	
box of cereal	
bag of flour	
bag of potato chips	
bag of onions	
jar of pickles	
jar of mayonnaise	
jar of jam	
basket of strawberries	
basket of apples	
six-pack of beer	
bottle of beer	
bottle of wine	
bottle of water	
2-liter bottle of soda	

✎ Phrase Practice 1

Fill in the blank with the correct container or unit.

1. We need to buy a_____ of wine.

2. This_____ of apples looks like a good one.

3. Can you help me open this_____ of jam?

4. You always buy a_____ of potato chips when we come to the store!

5. I need help reaching this_____ of cereal on the shelf.

6. Do we need a_____ of juice or do we have some at home?

7. Help me find a good_____ of grapes.

8. We need to get some_____ of meat from the deli.

9. I'm going to buy a_____ of bread at the corner store.

10. Will you pick up a_____ of beer on the way home?

ANSWER KEY
1. bottle; 2. basket; 3. jar; 4. bag; 5. box; 6. carton; 7. bunch; 8. slices; 9. loaf; 10. six-pack

Grammar Builder 1

▶ 10B Grammar Builder 1 (CD 5, Track 19)

THE SIMPLE PAST VS. THE PRESENT PERFECT

There are two common past tenses in English: the present perfect tense and the simple past tense. You learned the simple past tense in Lesson 5, and the present perfect tense in Lesson 9.

PRESENT PERFECT	SIMPLE PAST
I have spoken	I spoke
you have spoken	you spoke

PRESENT PERFECT	SIMPLE PAST
he/she/it has spoken	he/she/it spoke
we have spoken	we spoke
they have spoken	they spoke

These tenses are used differently. The present perfect tense is used:

a) for an event that happened in the past when the exact time is not known
b) when there's a result or connection being made to the present
c) when the time period is still unfinished (so far this week, up to now, during my life)

The simple past tense, on the other hand, is used for an action that happened when a specific finished time is given (yesterday, last week, in 2005).

Let's look at some examples of these tenses in use.

Sarah has returned from the grocery store. (present perfect: the specific time isn't important, just that Sarah is now home)	
Sarah returned from the grocery store last night at eight. (simple past: specific time, last night at eight, mentioned)	
Has Sarah ever gone to the grocery store? (present perfect: ever means during her life, which is still unfinished)	
Sarah went to the grocery store last week. (simple past: specific time)	

| Sarah has gone to the grocery store three times so far this week. (present perfect: the week is still unfinished) | |

When using these two tenses with an expression showing length of time, keep in mind their different meaning:

| I worked at Avery Foods for ten years. (simple past: I no longer work there.) | |
| I have worked at Avery Foods for ten years. (present perfect: I still work there.) | |

Since will only be used with the present perfect tense in the past, as it implies that the action is still occurring.

| I have worked at Avery Foods since 2002. | |

Work Out 1

Fill in the blank with the correct tense—either simple past or present perfect—of the verb given in parentheses.

1. They_____ married since 1992. (be)

2. They_____ married for twenty years before the divorce. (be)

3. She_____ to the bank twice today so far. (go)

4. Last night at 7:30, we_____ a movie. (see)

5. They_____ to France in 2005. (go)

6. He_____to France twice in his lifetime, and he's going again

next year. (**be**)

7. They_____a bestselling book. (**write**, unknown

time)

8. I_____ at Simple Technotronics for five years before getting my

new job. (**work**)

9. She_____ at this store since last year. (**shop**)

10. He_____ a car. (**buy**, finished time)

ANSWER KEY
1. have been; 2. were; 3. has gone; 4. saw; 5. went; 6. has been; 7. have written; 8. worked; 9. has
shopped; 10. bought

Phrase Builder 2

▶ 10C Phrase Builder 2 (CD 5, Track 20)

to make a deposit	
to make a withdrawal	
to make a bundle	
to make a mistake	
to make it to (an event)	
to make (something) out	
to make (something/someone) into	
to make (something/someone) over	
to make up	
to make a go of it	
to make do	
to make time	

to make a mountain out of a molehill	
to make the most out of it	

✎ Phrase Practice 2

Fill in the blank with the best phrase.

1. She was going to try to do it; she was_____.

2. I invested my money well and_____.

3. She is going to the bank to_____ so
   she'll have cash for tonight.

4. He doesn't have his glasses on, so he can't_____ the words on
   the screen.

5. She_____
   _____ by thinking the situation was worse than it was.

6. I_____ by adding the deposits wrong.

7. It's a bad situation, but we'll try to_____.

8. The store manager took the money from the registers and is going to the bank
   to_____.

9. We can't_____ the party tonight.

10. He_____ a story to get out of going to the party.

ANSWER KEY
1. making a go of it; 2. made a bundle; 3. make a withdrawal; 4. make out; 5. made a mountain out of
a molehill; 6. made a mistake; 7. make the most out of it; 8. make a deposit; 9. make it to; 10. made
up

Grammar Builder 2

▶ 10D Grammar Builder 2 (CD 5, Track 21)

THE PAST PROGRESSIVE

In Lesson 1, you learned that the present progressive is formed with the verb **to be** + the –**ing** form of the verb. Likewise, you now can learn that the past progressive is formed with the past tense of **to be** + the –**ing** form of the verb. Just like the present progressive, it describes a continuous action that was taking place at the time being spoken about, but one that took place in the past.

What were you doing yesterday?	
They were shopping at the store.	
I was buying chicken breasts for dinner.	

The past progressive is most often used to explain an action that was taking place when something else happened. When you introduce a new event that interrupts or takes places at the same time as the past progressive action, it will be in the simple past tense.

I was doing my homework when he came into the room.	
We were eating dinner when the doorbell rang.	
She was shopping for dinner when she remembered they needed salt.	
Their parents cleaned the kitchen while they were sleeping.	

Because these actions are continuous, the progressive tenses are sometimes called continuous tenses.

✎ Work Out 2

Fill in the blank with the correct tense (past progressive or past) of the verb given in parentheses.

1. She_____ her essay when he knocked on the door (**write**)

2. What were you doing yesterday when I_____? (**call**)

3. They_____ chicken breasts for dinner when they saw him across the street. (**buy**)

4. We_____ to the bank when our car broke down. (**go**)

5. I was taking out the trash when I_____ the raccoon. (**see**)

6. His parents_____ his bedroom while he was away last week. (**clean**)

7. He made a deposit at the bank while she_____ in the car. (**wait**)

8. Were you sleeping when I_____ to the house? (**come**)

9. They_____ down the street when they saw the accident. (**walk**)

10. Everyone_____ during the film. (**talk**)

ANSWER KEY

1. was writing; 2. called; 3. were buying; 4. were going; 5. saw; 6. cleaned; 7. was waiting; 8. came; 9. were walking; 10. was talking

✎ Drive It Home

Fill in the blank with the correct missing word.

1. She_____ planning last week for the party tonight.

2. He_____ writing his report when she called.

3. I_____ trying to open a bank account.

4. He_____ watching television, he was cooking.

5. She_____ driving yesterday, she was walking.

6. I_____ sleeping when you called.

7. They_____ depositing the checks.

8. We_____ doing our online banking when you called.

9. You_____ asking the teller about their types of checking accounts.

10. They_____ making a withdrawal.

ANSWER KEY
1-3 all was; 4-6 all wasn't; 7-10 all were

How Did You Do?

Let's see how you did in this lesson. By now, you should be able to:

☐ use container nouns for food such as **carton of eggs** and **loaf of bread** (Still unsure? Jump back to page 161.)

☐ understand the difference between the present perfect and the simple past (Still unsure? Jump back to page 162.)

☐ use expressions with the verb **make** (Still unsure? Jump back to page 165.)

☐ use the past progressive (**I was going**) (Still unsure? Jump back to page 167.)

✎ Word Recall

Match each container below in the left column with its best match in the right column.

1. carton	a. cheese
2. box	b. juice
3. jar	c. pickles
4. loaf	d. potato chips
5. bottle	e. wine
6. slice	f. bread
7. bunch	g. pasta
8. bag	h. grapes

ANSWER KEY
1. b; 2. g; 3. c; 4. f; 5. e; 6. a; 7. h; 8. d

Lesson 11: Sentences

In this lesson you'll learn:

☐ quantifiers such as **every, both, several, a few,** and **a little**

☐ how to form and use tag questions

Sentence Builder 1

▶ 11A Sentence Builder 1 (CD 5, Track 22)

Do you have any organic eggs?	
We need to get a lot of flour to make the cake.	

Many grocery stores have pharmacies.	
She's going to the store to get some milk.	
Several farmers markets are open year round.	
I need a few eggs for this recipe.	
Both stores sell what we're looking for.	
They bought every bottle of wine in the store.	
Try to fit the groceries into one bag if you can.	
They don't have any grapes left.	
The store had no bread left on the shelf.	
All food in this store is local.	

✎ Sentence Practice 1

Listen again to Sentence Builder 1 and fill in the missing words you hear below.

1. Do you have_____?

2. We need to get_____ to make the cake.

3. _____ have pharmacies.

4. She's going to the store to get_____.

5. _____ are open year round.

6. I need_____ for this recipe.

7. _____ sell what we're looking for.

8. They bought_____ in the store.

9. Try to fit the groceries into_____ if you can.

10. They don't have_____ left.

11. The store had_____ left on the shelf.

12. _____ in this store is organic.

ANSWER KEY
1. any eggs; 2. a lot of flour; 3. Many grocery stores; 4. some milk; 5. Several farmers markets; 6. a few eggs; 7. Both stores; 8. every bottle of wine; 9. one bag; 10. any grapes; 11. no bread; 12. All food

Grammar Builder 1

▶ 11B Grammar Builder 1 (CD 5, Track 23)

QUANTIFIERS

In English, words that answer the questions **how much** and **how many** are called quantifiers. Some quantifiers are only used with count nouns.

SINGULAR	
one One bag of groceries is all I can carry.	
every We need every egg you have.	
each Each aisle in the store has its own sign.	

PLURAL	
both **He went to both stores—Green's and Humbert's—looking for the items on his list.**	
a few **We need to get a few bottles of wine.**	
a couple of **There are a couple of eggs left in the fridge.**	
many **Many stores in this area are open twenty-four hours.**	
several **Several stores nearby sell specialty foods.**	

Some quantifiers are only used with noncount nouns.

much **Don't drink too much wine.**	
a little **I'll just have a little food before we go.**	

Other quantifiers can be used with either count or noncount nouns. Remember that these quantifiers will always be followed by count nouns in the plural.

some **Some grocery stores have an organic section.** **We need to get some food for the party.**	

a lot of **A lot of grocery stores have pharmacies.** **We need to get a lot of food for the party.**	
plenty of **There are plenty of grocery stores around here.** **We need to get plenty of food for the party.**	
all **All grocery stores have canned goods.** **All food cooked in this restaurant is organic.**	
most **Most grocery stores have a dairy section.** **Most food cooked in this restaurant is local.**	

In negative sentences, use **no**, **not any**, **none**, and **hardly any** with noncount nouns and plural count nouns.

no **We have no bananas.**	
not any **We don't have any bananas.**	
none **None of my friends are coming to the party.**	

hardly any **Hardly any people are coming to this party.**	

Any can also be used in questions with noncount nouns and plural count nouns.

Do we have any books? **– We don't have any books.** **– We have one book.** **– We have some books.** **– We have many books.**	
Do we have any milk? **– We don't have any milk.** **– We have a little milk.** **– We have some milk.** **– We have a lot of milk.**	

✎ Work Out 1

Choose the best quantifier to complete each sentence.

1. We don't have_____ milk.

   a. **no**

   b. **any**

   c. **some**

   d. **several**

2. They needed_____ bottles of wine for the party.

   a. **much**

   b. **several**

c. a little

d. none

3. _____ stores had what we were looking for.

a. Both

b. Any

c. Every

d. A little

4. Add_____ milk to your coffee.

a. many

b. several

c. a few

d. a little

5. She needs to get_____ eggs for the recipe.

a. much

b. a little

c. a couple of

d. not any

6. She looked in_____ store for the items on her list.

a. several

b. both

c. every

d. many

Intermediate English

7. There are_____ places we could go to get chicken breasts.

   a. **many**

   b. **each**

   c. **every**

   d. **one**

8. You can get_____ chicken breasts at the meat counter.

   a. **a little**

   b. **much**

   c. **some**

   d. **each**

9. Did you go to_____ flea markets when you were in France?

   a. **each**

   b. **every**

   c. **much**

   d. **many**

10. The farmers market had_____ canned food.

    a. **several**

    b. **no**

    c. **many**

    d. **a couple of**

ANSWER KEY
1. b; 2. b; 3. a; 4. d; 5. c; 6. c; 7. a; 8. c; 9. d; 10. b

Sentence Builder 2

▶ 11C Sentence Builder 2 (CD 5, Track 24)

Your bank has online banking, doesn't it?	
I can open a free checking account, can't I?	
They don't charge monthly fees for checking, do they?	
She's the new teller, isn't she?	
He speaks fluent Spanish, doesn't he?	
I have to set up automatic debit, don't I?	
This is the best interest rate, isn't it?	
Everyone at this bank is so friendly, aren't they?	
Nothing is ever free, is it?	
We paid our mortgage, didn't we?	
She will deposit the check, won't she?	
She didn't deposit the check, did she?	

✎ Sentence Practice 2

Listen again to Sentence Builder 2 and fill in the missing word or words that you hear.

1. Your bank has_____, doesn't it?

2. I can open a free checking account,_____?

3. They don't charge_____ for checking, do they?

4. She's the new teller,_____?

5. He speaks fluent Spanish,_____?

6. I have to set up_____, don't I?

7. This is the_____, isn't it?

8. Everyone at this bank is so friendly,_____?

9. Nothing is ever free,_____?

10. We paid our mortgage,_____?

11. She will_____, won't she?

12. She didn't deposit the check,_____?

ANSWER KEY
1. online banking; 2. can't I; 3. monthly fees; 4. isn't she; 5. doesn't he; 6. automatic debit; 7. best interest rate; 8. aren't they; 9. is it; 10. didn't we; 11. deposit the check; 12. did she

Grammar Builder 2
▶ 11D Grammar Builder 2 (CD 5, Track 25)

TAG QUESTIONS

Tag questions are used for confirmation, to seek agreement, or to express doubt or disapproval. Form tag questions by inverting the helping verb (do, be, have) and the subject, then negating it.

| You're going to the grocery store, aren't you? | |
| She's our new boss, isn't she? | |

He speaks Mandarin Chinese, doesn't he?	

Note that most sentences in the simple present use the helping verb do/does. (The negative of he speaks is he doesn't speak.) There are some exceptions to this that you'll see later in this grammar note.

If the statement is already negative, then the tag question will be positive.

They don't shop there, do they?	
We haven't been to this store before, have we?	

The tag question for sentences containing I am is aren't I?

I'm going to have a lot of work to do tonight, aren't I?	

If the sentence contains a modal verb such as can, could, would, should, or must, it will be repeated in the tag question ending.

We should buy some more paper towels, shouldn't we?	
You can come to my party tonight, can't you?	

If the sentence contains have to, has to, need to, or want to, use do or does (for third person singular) in the tag ending.

We have to go to the grocery store to get some more eggs, don't we?	
You need to be there at five, don't you?	
She has to buy milk, doesn't she?	

If the subject is **this**, **that**, **these**, or **those**, use **it** (singular) or **they** (plural) in the tag ending.

This is about a pound of broccoli, isn't it?	
That steak pairs well with this wine, doesn't it?	
These avocados are ripe, aren't they?	
Those nuts are a dollar per pound, aren't they?	

You will also use **it** for indefinite pronouns that refer to things, such as **everything**, **something**, or **anything**, and **they** for indefinite pronouns that refer to people, such as **everybody**, **everyone**, **someone**, or **anyone**.

Everything is so expensive here, isn't it?	
Everyone here is so happy all the time, aren't they?	

If the subject of the sentence is a negative word such as **nothing** or **no one**, or if **never** is used in the sentence, follow it with a positive tag ending.

Nothing here is fat free, is it?	
They never pay with cash, do they?	

Sentences in the simple past will use the helping verb **did** to form tag question endings (except for the verb **to be**); sentences in the simple future will use **will**.

They bought the last of the chicken breasts, didn't they?	
We were in France last year, weren't we?	
You'll take the trash out, won't you?	

✎ Work Out 2

Rewrite each statement below to include a tag question.

1. This bank uses online banking.

   _____

2. Everything is cheap here.

   _____

3. She can open a free checking account.

   _____

4. These are the best interest rates.

   _____

5. They aren't going to Italy.

   _____

6. You need to pay your mortgage.

   _____

7. He works at the bank.

   _____

8. I'm making a deposit after lunch.

   _____

9. We never go to that restaurant.

   _____

10. She has to close her account.

    _____

ANSWER KEY

1. This bank uses online banking, doesn't it? 2. Everything is cheap here, isn't it? 3. She can open a free checking account, can't she? 4. These are the best interest rates, aren't they? 5. They aren't going to Italy, are they? 6. You need to pay your mortgage, don't you? 7. He works at the bank, doesn't he? 8. I'm making a deposit after lunch, aren't I? 9. We never go to that restaurant, do we? 10. She has to close her account, doesn't she?

✎ Drive It Home

Finish the sentence with a tag question.

1. These apples taste great,_____?

2. They speak Russian,_____?

3. Everyone has to have a bank account,_____?

4. Those deposit slips need to be filled in,_____?

5. The grocery stores all have frozen food sections,_____?

6. These peaches aren't fresh,_____?

7. They aren't going to China next year,_____?

8. Sarah and John are never going to get married,_____?

9. Those people aren't waiting in line,_____?

10. Not everyone here is American,_____?

ANSWER KEY

1-5 all don't they; 6-10 all are they

How Did You Do?

Let's see how you did in this lesson. By now, you should be able to:

☐ use quantifiers such as every, both, several, a few, and a little (Still unsure? Jump back to page 172.)

☐ form and use tag questions (Still unsure? Jump back to page 179.)

✎ Word Recall

Give the past participle for the verbs below.

1. take _____

2. write _____

3. bring _____

4. eat _____

5. drink _____

6. know _____

7. make _____

8. work _____

9. got _____

10. go _____

ANSWER KEY
1. taken; 2. written; 3. brought; 4. eaten; 5. drunk; 6. known; 7. made; 8. worked; 9. gotten; 10. gone

Lesson 12: Conversations

By the end of this lesson, you should be able to:

☐ use **may** and **might** to express possibility

☐ use possessive pronouns (**mine, yours**) and the question word **whose?**

ᴬ Conversation 1

▶ 12A Conversation 1 (CD 5, Track 26)

Angela and Brian have invited some friends over for dinner, so they're at a supermarket shopping for food. Listen in.

Angela:	What else is on the list?
Brian:	Let's see . . . we've gotten the onions, tomatoes, garlic, basil, and a box of pasta. Here's a carton of milk, a dozen eggs, and some cheese. Why do we need the eggs? We're cooking pasta and chicken, aren't we?
Angela:	Yes, we are, but we're out of eggs. You were just saying that you feel like French toast for breakfast tomorrow.
Brian:	Oh, yeah. I was saying that, wasn't I?
Angela:	What else on the list haven't we gotten?
Brian:	We still need the meat, the bread, the wine, and some ice cream for dessert.
Angela:	I bought a bottle of wine the other day. And Sam and Pete will probably bring wine.
Brian:	But there will be seven of us. Two bottles may not be enough. Especially if people are staying late.
Angela:	But Anna will probably bring a bottle, too.

Brian:	Yeah, she never buys decent wine. We might want to pick up another bottle just to be safe, in case hers is no good.
Angela:	Okay, fine, although please don't tell our guest that her wine is not as good as ours. So we need the meat, a few loaves of bread, and some ice cream.
Brian:	Wait, didn't you say that Pete is bringing dessert? We were walking to the car when you got a text message from him. You told me that he was baking a cake.
Angela:	He was baking a cake. He texted me while it was baking, in fact. But he asked me to get ice cream to serve with the cake.
Brian:	Oh, great idea! Vanilla, please.
Angela:	So, now, we still haven't gotten the chicken. Could you go to the meat counter and get some chicken breasts? I'll go to the bakery and get a couple of loaves of bread.
Brian:	Great. And then we'll have every item on the list.
Angela:	Meet me at the register. And Brian, just chicken. No potato chips. Every time we come here you pick up a bag of potato chips.
Brian:	But the snacks are on the way to the meat counter!
Angela:	On second thought, you go get the bread, and I'll get the chicken instead.

✎ Conversation Practice 1

Answer the following questions based on the dialogue.

1. Which of these is not on the original list: a dozen eggs, a carton of milk, tomatoes, a loaf of bread.

_____

2. Why do Angela and Brian need eggs?

_____

3. What does Brian feel like having for breakfast tomorrow?

_____

4. What do they need for dessert?

_____

5. How many bottles of wine will they have, not including Anna's?

_____

6. Who is bringing dessert?

_____

7. What is this person going to do for dessert?

_____

8. What does Angela tell Brian to get at the meat counter?

_____

9. Where is Angela going to get the loaves of bread?

_____

10. Where are they going to meet after they get what they need?

_____

ANSWER KEY
1. A loaf of bread is not on the original list. 2. They're out of eggs. 3. He feels like having French toast. 4. They need ice cream for dessert. 5. They will have three bottles of wine. 6. Pete is bringing dessert. 7. Pete is baking a cake for dessert. 8. She tells him to get chicken breasts. 9. Angela is going to get the loaves of bread at the bakery. 10. They are going to meet at the register.

Grammar Builder 1

▶ 12B Grammar Builder 1 (CD 5, Track 27)

POSSIBILITY WITH MAY AND MIGHT

May and might are two words used to express possibility. May and might can be used in the same way. For some speakers, may is used for a slightly stronger possibility than might, but don't worry too much about this difference.

I may open a bank account./I might open a bank account.	
It may rain tomorrow./It might rain tomorrow.	

In the past tense, you will use may have/might have + the past participle.

We may have charged you too much.	
She might have been there last night.	

In the future tense, you will use may be/might be + the –ing form of the verb.

The interest rates may be increasing over the next quarter.	
She might be coming in late to work today.	

✎ Work Out 1

Change the tense of the sentence based on the clue in parentheses.

1. We might see her tomorrow. (yesterday)

_____

Intermediate English

2. He may be about to get here. (last Tuesday)

_____

3. It might snow. (next week)

_____

4. I may have the information you need. (last week)

_____

5. She might see the film. (last night)

_____

6. We may charge you too much. (yesterday)

_____

7. They might go to China. (next year)

_____

8. You may receive a letter from us in the mail. (next week)

_____

9. Sheila and George may write this report. (last week)

_____

10. I might take your phone by mistake. (this morning)

_____

ANSWER KEY

1. We might have seen her yesterday. 2. He may have been about to get here last Tuesday. 3. It might be snowing next week./It might snow next week. 4. I may have had the information you needed last week. 5. She might have seen the film last night. 6. We may have charged you too much yesterday. 7. They might be going to China next year./They might go to China next year. 8. You may be receiving a letter from us in the mail next week./You may receive a letter from us in the mail next week. 9. Sheila and George may have written this report last week. 10. I might have taken your phone by mistake this morning.

🎧 Conversation 2

▶ 12C Conversation 2 (CD 5, Track 28)

Troy Collins has just moved into a new town, so he needs to open a bank account.
Listen in.

Troy:	Hi there. My name is Troy Collins. I want to talk to someone about opening a bank account.
Bank Teller:	Of course, Mr. Collins. Here's a brochure that will tell you about the different types of accounts we have to offer. You can have a seat and take a look at that. Someone will be with you in just a few minutes.
Troy:	Okay, thanks.
Stephanie:	Mr. Collins? Hi, I'm Stephanie Meyers. I understand that you want to open an account with us?
Troy:	Yes, that's right.
Stephanie:	Come on into my office, and I can help you with that. Here we are. Please have a seat.
Troy:	Thank you.
Stephanie:	So, have you done banking with us before?
Troy:	No, I've just moved here from out of state. I did a little research online, and it seems like this bank will be convenient for me.
Stephanie:	Welcome to the area! We might not be the biggest bank in the country, but we have about twenty branches in the region, and very competitive interest rates. Are you looking for investment services, a business account, or personal checking and savings accounts?
Troy:	Just basic personal checking and savings. I was reading your brochure, and I see that you offer free checking and basic checking. What's the difference?

Stephanie: There are actually a few other types of checking accounts, and the differences really come down to whether you want to keep a minimum balance and what other services you need. Our basic account is called "Totally Free Checking," and with that type of account, there's no minimum monthly balance and no monthly fee.

Troy: Sounds good. So what don't I get with that?

Stephanie: Well, there's no interest, which may not be a problem if you also plan on opening a savings account, but there's also a per-check fee that kicks in after you've written five checks in one month.

Troy: I see. I don't write many checks. I've paid most of my monthly bills—mortgage, car payments, etc.—by automatic debit each month. You offer that, don't you?

Stephanie: We do with our "Premiere e-Checking" account. There's no fee for checks if you decide to write them, and there's a competitive interest rate. You can also do all of your banking online. But there is a small monthly fee if your balance drops below the minimum balance of $1,000.

Troy: Hmmm ... I see that you offer quite a few different types of checking accounts, don't you? I'm going to take this information home and decide which one is best for me. Can I call you if I have questions?

Stephanie: Of course. Here's my card. I'm happy to answer any questions you may have. When you've decided what you like, just come back in, and we'll have some forms for you to fill out. We'll need a driver's license and your social security number, just the usual personal information.

Troy: Okay, thanks for your help, and I'll be in touch in the next few days.

Stephanie: Thank you, Mr. Collins. We look forward to banking with you.

✎ Conversation Practice 2

Answer the following questions based on the dialogue.

1. What does Troy want to do at the bank?

   _____

2. Has Troy done banking with this bank before? Why or why not?

   _____

3. How many branches of the bank are in the area?

   _____

4. What types of accounts is Troy interested in?

   _____

5. What two types of checking does the bank offer according to the brochure?

   _____

6. What is "Totally Free Checking"?

   _____

7. When does the per-check fee kick in with "Totally Free Checking"?

   _____

8. How does Troy pay his mortgage and car payments?

   _____

9. When would Troy be charged a small monthly fee with "Premiere e-Checking"?

   _____

10. What two things does the bank need from Troy to open an account?

ANSWER KEY

1. He wants to open a bank account. 2. No, because he just moved to the area from out of state. 3. There are twenty branches of the bank. 4. Troy is interested in basic personal checking and savings. 5. The brochure says that the bank offers free checking and basic checking. 6. "Totally Free Checking" is a basic account with no minimum monthly balance and no monthly fee. 7. The per-check fee kicks in after you've written five checks in one month. 8. Troy pays his mortgage and car payments with automatic debit. 9. Troy would be charged a small monthly fee if his balance drops below the minimum balance of $1,000. 10. The bank needs his driver's license and his social security number.

Grammar Builder 2

▶ 12D Grammar Builder 2 (CD 5, Track 29)

POSSESSIVE PRONOUNS AND WHOSE

You already learned that possessive adjectives (my, your, his, hers, etc.) are used with nouns to describe something that belongs to someone. Possessive pronouns are used in place of these nouns to answer the question whose?

Their bank is the best bank in the city. Whose (bank) is the best bank in the city? Theirs is the best bank in the city.	
Our interest rate will remain stable. Whose (interest rate) will remain stable? Ours will remain stable.	

These are the possessive pronouns:

mine	ours
yours	yours
his/hers/its	theirs

Let's take a look at more possessive pronouns in use. Note that the possessive pronoun doesn't change whether it's the subject or the object of a sentence.

Whose towel is this? It's mine.	
Is this their car? No, it's ours.	
His is the red one.	
Yours is broken; let's take mine.	

With proper nouns, the answer to **whose?** is just the proper noun with an **'s.**

Whose book are you reading? Sharon's.	
Ours is the striped one; Mr. Brown's is the solid one.	

Take It Further
MORE ON APOSTROPHE S

Even English speakers sometimes have a hard time properly using an apostrophe s.

Remember that you use **it's** for **it is**. **Its** is a possessive pronoun that doesn't take an apostrophe s.

When forming possessives with proper nouns ending in an s, you can either add an apostrophe s or just an apostrophe.

James's/James' bank is closed on Sundays.	
Mr. Hughes's/Mr. Hughes' shoes are brown.	

For plural nouns ending in s, use only an apostrophe with no s.

The wives' husbands were having lunch.	
The girls' room needs to be cleaned.	

When a plural noun doesn't end in an s, you should use an apostrophe s to create a possessive: men's, children's.

The apostrophe s is also often used with abbreviated words—CD's, DVD's, IPO's—though many people still write these words without apostrophes.

✎ Work Out 2

Answer the questions below in complete sentences using possessive pronouns based on the clues in parentheses.

1. Whose shirt is this? (my shirt)

   _____

2. Whose checkbook is that? (it belongs to Angela)

   _____

3. Whose room is this? (**our room**)

_____

4. Whose wine is this? (**their wine**)

_____

5. Whose car is this? (**her car**)

_____

6. Whose car is the red one? (**his car**)

_____

7. Whose pen is this? (**it belongs to James**)

_____

8. Whose bank account has the most money? (**my bank account**)

_____

9. Whose bank has the highest interest rates? (**our bank**)

_____

10. Whose house is bigger, my house or your house? (**my house**)

_____

ANSWER KEY
1. This shirt is mine./It's mine. 2. That checkbook is Angela's./It's Angela's. 3. This room is ours./
It's ours. 4. This wine is theirs./It's theirs. 5. This car is hers./It's hers. 6. The red car is his. /His is
the red one. 7. This pen is James's/James'./It's James's/James'. 8. The bank account with the most
money is mine./Mine has the most money. 9. The bank with the highest interest rates is ours./
Ours has the highest interest rates. 10. The bigger house is mine./Mine is bigger than yours.

Intermediate English

✎ Drive It Home

Form questions from the sentences below using **whose?**

1. This shirt is mine.

   _____

2. This checkbook is Angela's.

   _____

3. This bank is ours.

   _____

4. This shopping cart is theirs.

   _____

5. This cake is hers.

   _____

6. This pen is yours.

   _____

7. This red car is his.

   _____

8. Theirs is the blue car.

   _____

9. Ours is the highest interest rate.

   _____

10. Mine is the bigger house.

   _____

ANSWER KEY
1. Whose shirt is this? 2. Whose checkbook is this? 3. Whose bank is this? 4. Whose shopping car is this? 5. Whose cake is this? 6. Whose pen is this? 7. Whose is this red car? 8. Whose is the blue car? 9. Whose is the highest interest rate? 10. Whose is the bigger house?

Take It Further
HIGHER NUMBERS

Now that you know some vocabulary for dealing with banks, you may also want to know how to form numbers above 100. To get 100, 200, 300, 400, etc. place a number (one, two, three, four) in front of hundred. The tens come after separated by and.

one hundred/a hundred	100
one hundred and one/a hundred and one	101
one hundred and two/a hundred and two	102
one hundred and three/a hundred and three	103
one hundred and forty-two/a hundred and forty-two	142
two hundred	200
three hundred	300
four hundred	400
five hundred and ninety-five	595
six hundred and eighty-eight	688

When counting a sequence, you may hear people leave out the and in higher numbers: one hundred one, one hundred two, one hundred three ... two hundred thirteen, two hundred fourteen, two hundred fifteen ... But you won't hear the and left out when using a hundred: a hundred and one, a hundred and two, a hundred and three.

After nine-hundred and ninety-nine (999), you have the thousands. Again, just place a number before thousand, and the hundreds and tens follow.

one thousand/a thousand	1,000
one thousand and one/a thousand and one	1,001
two thousand	2,000
three thousand	3,000
ten thousand	10,000
twenty thousand	20,000
thirty-four thousand, three hundred and forty-two	34,342
one hundred thousand/a hundred thousand	100,000
three hundred thousand	300,000
four hundred sixty-one thousand, two hundred and eleven	461,211

Note that the and only comes before the tens in these more complex numbers.

After nine hundred ninety-nine thousand nine hundred and ninety-nine (999,999), you have the millions, billions, and trillions.

one million/a million	1,000,000
one billion/a billion	1,000,000,000
one trillion/a trillion	1,000,000,000,000

Unit 3 Lesson 12: Conversations

If you want to talk specifically about American money, use **dollars** and **cents**.

We have five hundred twenty-seven dollars and twenty-five cents ($527.25) in our bank account.	
They received a bill for thirteen thousand seven hundred fifty dollars and eighty-nine cents ($13,750.89).	
The national debt currently stands at over fifteen trillion dollars.	

Note as well that when writing numerals, a comma is used to separate the thousands and millions, while a period is used to separate the decimals.

How Did You Do?

Let's see how you did in this lesson. By now, you should be able to:

☐ use **may** and **might** to express possibility (Still unsure? Jump back to page 188.)

☐ use possessive pronouns (**mine, yours**) and the question word **whose?** (Still unsure? Jump back to page 193.)

✎ Word Recall

Give the possessive pronoun for the objects below.

1. her house _____

2. our bank _____

3. my checkbook _____

4. James's savings account _____

5. their car _____

6. your hat _____

7. his apple_____

8. my book and your book _____

ANSWER KEY

1. **hers**; 2. **ours**; 3. **mine**; 4. **James's/his**; 5. **theirs**; 6. **yours**; 7. **his**; 8. **mine** and **yours/ours**

Don't forget to practice and reinforce what you've learned by visiting **www.livinglanguage.com/ languagelab** for flashcards, games, and quizzes!

Unit 3 Quiz

Let's put the most essential English words and grammar points you've learned so far to practice in a few exercises. It's important to be sure that you've mastered this material before you move on. Score yourself at the end of the review and see if you need to go back for more practice, or if you're ready to move on to Unit 4.

A. Fill in the blanks below with the correct tense of the verb shown in parentheses.

1. We_____ this car since 1992. (**have**)

2. She_____ across the country from March to August last year. (**drive**)

3. They_____ us about their trip yet. (**not tell**)

4. _____ any cleaning so far? (**do, they**)

B. Choose the correct tense of the verb in parentheses to fill in the blank in each sentence below.

1. We_____ errands when you called. (**run**)

2. What were you reading yesterday when I_____ you? (**see**)

3. While I_____ for you, a friend of mine walked past me.

   (**wait**)

4. When you_____ to them yesterday, were they feeling okay? (**speak**)

C. Circle the correct missing quantifier.

1. We need (**a few/a little**) eggs to bake this cake.

2. (**All/Each**) grocery stores will have the ingredients you need.

3. There isn't (**many/much**) milk left in the house.

D. Rewrite the sentences below with tag questions.

1. He speaks Chinese really well.

_____

2. You're not listening.

_____

3. We could go to the movies.

_____

4. This trash needs to be taken out.

_____

E. Rewrite the sentences below to express possibility.

1. We will see you tomorrow.

_____

2. They were out of town last week.

_____

F. Answer the questions using possessive pronouns based on the clue in parentheses.

1. Whose shopping cart is this? (**her shopping cart**)

_____

2. Whose milk is this? (**my milk**)

_____

ANSWER KEY

A. 1. have had; 2. drove; 3. haven't told; 4. Have they done
B. 1. were running; 2. saw; 3. was waiting; 4. spoke
C. 1. a few; 2. All; 3. much
D. 1. He speaks Chinese really well, doesn't he? 2. You're not listening, are you? 3. We could go to the movies, couldn't we? 4. This trash needs to be taken out, doesn't it?
E. 1. We may/might be seeing you tomorrow. 2. They may/might have been out of town last week.
F. 1. It's hers. 2. It's mine.

How Did You Do?

Give yourself a point for every correct answer, then use the following key to tell whether you're ready to move on:

0–7 points: It's probably a good idea to go back through the lesson again. You may be moving too quickly, or there may be too much "down time" between your contact with English. Remember that it's better to spend 30 minutes with English three or four times a week than it is to spend two or three hours just once a week. Find a pace that's comfortable for you, and spread your contact hours out as much as you can.

8–12 points: You would benefit from a review before moving on. Go back and spend a little more time on the specific points that gave you trouble. Re-read the Grammar Builder sections that were difficult, and do the work out one more time. Don't forget about the online supplemental practice material, either. Go to **www.livinglanguage.com/languagelab** for games and quizzes that will reinforce the material from this unit.

13–17 points: Good job! There are just a few points that you could consider reviewing before moving on. If you haven't worked with the games and quizzes on **www.livinglanguage.com/languagelab**, please give them a try.

18–20 points: Great! You're ready to move on to the next unit.

 points

Unit 4:
On the Phone

Welcome to Unit 4! This unit is all about using the telephone. You'll learn important vocabulary to help you make appointments and talk to customer service. You'll also learn useful phrases like **hold on**, and **call back**, which are very common in English.

Additionally, you'll learn how to use participles as adjectives (**written, cancelled**), use the present tense to talk about the future with **if, when**, and **as soon as**, and how to use modals such as **ought, supposed to**, and **had better**. Finally, you'll learn how to make suggestions and ask for permission using **let's** and how to use the impersonal **one, you**, and **they** to talk generally about something.

Ready?

Lesson 13: Words
In this lesson you'll learn:

☐ vocabulary for talking on the telephone and making appointments

☐ how to form and use participial adjectives (**damaging, damaged**)

☐ customer service vocabulary

☐ how to use the present tense to talk about the future with **if, when, as soon as**

Participial Adjectives

Phrasal Verbs and
Prepositional Verbs

The Future Expressed
by the Present

Separable Phrasal Verbs

Word Builder 1

▶ 13A Word Builder 1 (CD 6, Track 1)

telephone, phone, cell phone, mobile phone, wireless phone, smart phone, flip phone, touch-tone phone, landline	
call, call back, dial, put someone on hold, hang up, disconnect	
dial tone, busy signal, call-waiting signal	
appointment, schedule, calendar, reminder	
check-up, cleaning, filling, emergency, physical	
text message, text, predictive text, smiley, voicemail	
contacts, ring tone	
leave a message, send a text, hold the line	

✎ Word Practice 1

Fill in the blank with the appropriate missing word or words from Word Builder 1.

1. He likes his_____ because it lets him access the

   Internet when he's not near a computer.

2. If you want to see a dentist, you have to make an_____ first.

3. When you pick up a landline phone, the noise you hear before you call someone is

    the_____.

4. If someone isn't home when you call, you can_____

    to let him or her know that you called.

5. When you don't want to talk to someone on the phone but need to convey

    information to them, you can_____ instead.

6. If you call someone but they are on the phone with someone else, you will

    sometimes hear a_____.

7. On most mobile phones, you can choose a_____, or the sound

    a phone makes when someone calls you.

8. Put your appointments on the_____.

9. Set up a_____ to let you know when your appointments are.

10. You should go to the dentist for regular_____.

ANSWER KEY

1. smart phone; 2. appointment; 3. dial tone; 4. leave a message; 5. send a text; 6. busy signal; 7. ring
tone; 8. calendar; 9. reminder; 10. cleanings

Grammar Builder 1

▶ 13B Grammar Builder 1 (CD 6, Track 2)

PARTICIPIAL ADJECTIVES

The present participle (–ing) and past participles (–ed or irregular participle) can
both be used as adjectives. These are called participial adjectives.

Here's the sentence that is confusing.	
Here's the <u>confusing</u> sentence.	

Participial Adjectives

Phrasal Verbs and
Prepositional Verbs

The Future Expressed
by the Present

Separable Phrasal Verbs

This is the object that was found. This is the <u>found</u> object.	

They each have different meanings when used as adjectives. The present participle used as an adjective is active and describes an action happening during the time of the sentence.

There are damaging rumors being spread around about our candidate.	
She heard a cracking sound when she bit into the olive pit.	
I felt a shooting pain in my left arm.	
These noise-cancelling headphones are really good for work.	

The past participle used as an adjective is passive and describes something that happened to the noun it is modifying in the past. (Don't forget the irregular past participles!)

The damaged tooth had to be removed.	
I have a cracked tooth from when I bit into an olive pit.	
Can you smell that burnt toast?	
We can reschedule your cancelled appointment.	

Tip: Remember that the present participial adjective describes something being modified in the present, while the past participial adjective describes something that was modified in the past.

✎ Work Out 1

Fill in the blank with the correct participial adjective based on the clue in parentheses.

1. They all met at the airport to greet the_____ soldier. (return, present)

2. We can try to reschedule your_____ appointment for next Tuesday. (cancel, past)

3. The earth travels around the sun; this is a_____ fact. (know, past)

4. Did you hear that_____ sound as the tree fell? (crack, present)

5. You can't use this_____ coupon. (expire, past)

6. They negotiated and agreed that it was a_____ deal. (do, past)

7. He planted a tree in her honor; it was a_____ tribute to her love of nature. (fit, present)

8. Be careful driving home; there are a lot of_____ drivers on the road. (drink, past)

9. She has an_____ pain in her tooth. (ache, present)

10. We have a_____ contract for our phone plan. (write, past)

ANSWER KEY
1. returning; 2. cancelled; 3. known; 4. cracking; 5. expired; 6. done; 7. fitting; 8. drunk; 9. aching; 10. written

Participial Adjectives

Phrasal Verbs and
Prepositional Verbs

The Future Expressed
by the Present

Separable Phrasal Verbs

Word Builder 2

▶ 13C Word Builder 2 (CD 6, Track 3)

customer service, customer service line, customer support, call center, billing department	
menu options, star (*), pound (#), PIN	
press, hold, transfer, wait	
customer, operator, representative, supervisor, technician	
existing customer, business customer, valued customer, cherished customer	
received, changed, activated, automated, applied	
unlimited, upgraded, paid	
service, account, data plan, voice plan, bill, activation, contract, coverage, overage fees	
unique, memorable, common, easy to remember	

✎ Word Practice 2

Fill in the blank with the appropriate missing word or words from Word Builder 2.

1. You need to_____ 0 to speak to the operator.

2. When you need to talk to someone about your phone plan, you can

   call_____.

3. When you want to talk to someone about your phone bill, you can call

   the_____.

4. You already have an account with this company, so you are

   an_____.

5. When you switch your account from a basic plan to a plan with more coverage,

   you have_____ your account.

6. You need to select a PIN that is_____, meaning you can

   remember it easily.

7. A_____ is the plan that allows you to access the Internet and

   download files on your phone.

8. If you have a plan that allows_____ text messages, you can

   send as many texts as you want.

9. When your account is_____, you can start using your phone.

10. If the customer service representative can't help you, they

    might_____ you to their supervisor.

ANSWER KEY
1. **press**; 2. **customer service**; 3. **billing department**; 4. **existing customer**; 5. **upgraded**; 6.
memorable; 7. **data plan**; 8. **unlimited**; 9. **activated**; 10. **transfer**

Participial Adjectives

Phrasal Verbs and
Prepositional Verbs

The Future Expressed
by the Present

Separable Phrasal Verbs

Grammar Builder 2

▶ 13D Grammar Builder 2 (CD 6, Track 4)

THE FUTURE EXPRESSED BY THE PRESENT

You already learned in Lesson 7 that the present progressive can be used to talk about the future.

What are you doing tomorrow night?	

The simple present tense can also be used to talk about the future when a specific schedule is involved.

We sail tomorrow at 9 a.m.	
They leave for Spain on Saturday.	
The train departs at 11.	

The simple present tense is also used to talk about future events in clauses that begin with conjunctions like when, as soon as, and if. The verbs in these clauses will be in the simple present tense, even though they refer to future events; the verb in the main clause will be in the future tense.

As soon as I get to the house, I will call the babysitter.	
When we are in Rome, we will do as Romans do.	
If she goes to the store, she'll buy some toilet paper.	

These sentences also work if the if/as soon as/when clause comes second.

I will call the babysitter as soon as I get to the house.	
We will do as Romans do when we are in Rome.	

She'll buy some toilet paper if she goes to the store.	

✎ Work Out 2

Combine the two sentences below into one sentence using the clues in parentheses. Don't forget to make sure the clauses are in the correct tense.

1. We go to France. We go to the Louvre. (**if**)

   _____

2. They get home. They make dinner. (**as soon as**)

   _____

3. You activate your account. You are able to use your cell phone. (**as soon as**)

   _____

4. He comes back to the hotel. We go down to the restaurant. (**when**)

   _____

5. You call customer service. They are able to help you. (**if**)

   _____

6. She is in town. We see a play on Broadway. (**when**)

   _____

7. Your tooth is cracked. You feel a shooting pain. (**if**)

   _____

8. I have a day off. I visit the dentist. (**as soon as**)

   _____

Participial Adjectives

Phrasal Verbs and
Prepositional Verbs

The Future Expressed
by the Present

Separable Phrasal Verbs

9. You run out of minutes. You are charged overage fees. (as soon as)

_____

10. He needs unlimited texting. He upgrades his account. (when)

_____

ANSWER KEY
1. If we go to France, we will go to the Louvre./We will go to the Louvre if we go to France. 2. As soon as they get home, they will make dinner./They will make dinner as soon as they get home. 3. As soon as you activate your account, you will be able to use your cell phone./You will be able to use your cell phone as soon as you activate your account. 4. When he comes back to the hotel, we'll go down to the restaurant./We'll go down to the restaurant when he comes back to the hotel. 5. If you call customer service, they will be able to help you./Customer service will be able to help you if you call them. 6. When she is in town, we will see a play on Broadway./We will see a play on Broadway when she is in town. 7. If your tooth is cracked, you will feel a shooting pain./You will feel a shooting pain if your tooth is cracked. 8. As soon as I have a day off, I will visit the dentist./I will visit the dentist as soon as I have a day off. 9. As soon as you run out of minutes, you will be charged overage fees./You will be charged overage fees as soon as you run out of minutes. 10. When he needs unlimited texting, he will upgrade his account./He will upgrade his account when he needs unlimited texting.

✎ Drive It Home

Change the clue in parentheses into a participial adjective to fill in the blank in each question below.

1. your_____ account (that was upgraded)

2. my_____ tooth (that was cracked)

3. her_____ foot (that was injured)

4. his_____ reputation (that was damaged)

5. our_____ friend (who was drunk)

6. their_____ tribute (that is fitting)

7. the tree's_____ noise (that is creaking)

8. a_____ smell (**that is burning**)

9. a_____ thought (**that is disturbing**)

10. my_____ head (**that is aching**)

ANSWER KEY
1. upgraded; 2. cracked; 3. injured; 4. damaged; 5. drunk; 6. fitting; 7. creaking; 8. burning;
9. disturbing; 10. aching

How Did You Do?

Let's see how you did in this lesson. By now, you should be able to:

☐ use vocabulary to talk on the telephone and make appointments (Still unsure? Jump back to page 206.)

☐ form and use participial adjectives (**damaging, damaged**) (Still unsure? Jump back to page 207.)

☐ use customer service vocabulary (Still unsure? Jump back to page 210.)

☐ use the present tense to talk about the future with **if, when, as soon as** (Still unsure? Jump back to page 212.)

✎ Word Recall

Match each word below in the left column to its best match in the right column.

1. cell phone	a. appointment
2. data plan	b. contract
3. calendar	c. voice plan
4. customer support	d. busy signal
5. dial tone	e. check-up
6. cleaning	f. representative
7. bill	g. wait
8. hold	h. mobile phone

Participial Adjectives

Phrasal Verbs and
Prepositional Verbs

The Future Expressed
by the Present

Separable Phrasal Verbs

ANSWER KEY
1. h; 2. c; 3. a; 4. f; 5. d; 6. e; 7. b; 8. g

Lesson 14: Phrases

In this lesson you'll learn:

☐ phrasal verbs, both separable (hang up) and inseparable (come back)

☐ phrasal verbs with get

☐ phrasal verbs with back

Phrase Builder 1

▶ 14A Phrase Builder 1 (CD 6, Track 5)

break down	
break up	
catch on	
check in/into	
check out	
check up	
come back	
deal with	
fall down	
fall through	
get by	
get in/into	
get off	

get on	
get out (of)	
get over	
get up	
go away	
hold on	
look after	
look out	
run into	
run out	
show up	
stand up	
take care of	
take off	
wake up	
wear off	

✎ Phrase Practice 1

Fill in the blanks with the correct phrase from Phrase Builder 1.

1. To_____ means to stand from a rising position, or to rise from bed in

   the morning.

2. To_____ for someone means to try to see them or find them.

3. When you_____ something, you stop being angry or otherwise

   emotional about something.

Participial Adjectives

Phrasal Verbs and
Prepositional Verbs

The Future Expressed
by the Present

Separable Phrasal Verbs

4. You_____ a problem, meaning you do what you can to make the problem stop.

5. When you_____ to somewhere, it means you return to somewhere you were before.

6. When you tell someone to_____ to something, you are either asking them to keep it for a while, or asking them to grab something tightly with their fist.

7. You can_____ someone by seeing them unexpectedly, without previous plans.

8. After you_____ in the morning, you usually get out of bed.

9. You_____ to an event, meaning you go to an event in person.

10. You_____ a car, but you get on a bus.

ANSWER KEY
1. get up; 2. look out; 3. get over; 4. deal with; 5. come back; 6. hold on; 7. run into; 8. wake up; 9. show up; 10. get in

Grammar Builder 1
▶ 14B Grammar Builder 1 (CD 6, Track 6)

PHRASAL VERBS AND PREPOSITIONAL VERBS

Phrasal verbs are verbs in English that are paired with prepositions or adverbs—called "particles" —that give the verb a new meaning. Phrasal verbs are conjugated just like their main verb, but the meaning is often very different from the meaning of the main verb. Phrasal verbs are common in English; you will have to memorize their meaning as you come across each phrasal verb, as some have several meanings, or are used in different ways. For example, you can **run out of** a room (leave a room quickly), for example, or you can run out of gas (exhaust your supply of gasoline, or, idiomatically, get tired).

There are two main types of phrasal verbs: separable and inseparable. We'll look at inseparable phrasal verbs first.

INSEPARABLE PHRASAL VERBS

Inseparable phrasal verbs are verbs in which the main verb and its particle cannot be separated by an object.

run into She ran into Shira the other day at the store.	
check into We'll check into the hotel before we go to the museum.	
check out We went to the museum to check out the Dalí exhibit.	
deal with She will deal with your problem when she is done dealing with mine.	
fall down Be careful not to fall down the stairs!	
look after While we were gone, our neighbors agreed to look after our cats.	

take care of He took care of his daughter when she was sick by making her chicken noodle soup.	

INTRANSITIVE PHRASAL VERBS

Some inseparable phrasal verbs are also intransitive, meaning they aren't followed by a direct object. Intransitive phrasal verbs can be followed by an indirect object.

break down The car broke down on the way to work, so he had to walk the rest of the way.	
break up I was shocked to hear that Shira and James broke up; they were such a great couple.	
catch on They had to be told the story three times before they caught on to who the murderer was.	
check up You should check up on the boys to make sure they're behaving.	
come back She came back to the store because she had left her wallet.	
fall through Our plans fell through, so we were left with nothing to do on Saturday night.	

hold on **Hold on to this record until I come back to get it./Hold on to this rope when you climb down the wall.**	
look out **Look out for me; I'll be the one wearing a red dress.**	
run out **We ran out of flour; will you pick some up at the store?**	
show up **By the time they showed up to the theater, it was too late to buy tickets.**	
stand up **Stand up so I can see how tall you are.**	
take off **The plane took off from the runway.**	
wake up **I woke up when my alarm sounded.**	
wear off **The numbing effects of the novocaine wore off and my teeth started to hurt again.**	

Keep in mind that some of these phrasal verbs are transitive and even separable when they have a different meaning. For example, while break up meaning "to end a relationship" is inseparable and intransitive, break up meaning "to split" is separable and transitive: They broke the fight up before it got out of hand. You can also stand up (rise to a standing position), or you can stand someone up (not go to a pre-arranged meeting or date). Another example is take off: when you are

Participial Adjectives

Phrasal Verbs and
Prepositional Verbs

The Future Expressed
by the Present

Separable Phrasal Verbs

talking about a plane leaving the ground or someone leaving very fast (**the dog took off before I could catch up**), the phrasal verb is inseparable and intransitive, but when you are **taking off your coat**, the verb is separable and transitive.

Be careful to study both the meaning of different phrasal verbs, as well as whether they are inseparable or separable. We'll look at separable phrasal verbs in Grammar Builder 2 of this lesson.

Take It Further
PHRASAL VERBS WITH GET

In Phrase Builder 1, you saw a lot of phrasal verbs with get. Let's look at how a few of them are used in sentences. We'll also note whether they're transitive or intransitive.

TRANSITIVE	
get in Get in the car and I'll drive you to the station.	
get into She got into all of the schools she applied to.	
get off Get off the couch! Your shoes are dirty.	
get on Get on the bus before the doors shut and it leaves you behind!	

Note that there are subtle differences between **get in** and **get on** when used with transportation; you can **get in** a car or a van, but you **get on** a bus, a train, a plane, a horse, or a bike.

INTRANSITIVE	
get by **We don't have much money, but we can get by on very little.**	
get out **When they got out of the subway, they saw that it was raining.**	
get up **I got up, got dressed, and went to the kitchen for breakfast.**	

✎ Work Out 1

Choose the correct phrasal verb that best completes each sentence.

1. When he_____ for his appointment, the dentist was already

   waiting for him.

   a. **checked up**

   b. **stood up**

   c. **showed up**

   d. **broke up**

2. Their babysitter_____ last minute and so we had to

   reschedule our dinner.

   a. **fell through**

Participial Adjectives

Phrasal Verbs and
Prepositional Verbs

The Future Expressed
by the Present

Separable Phrasal Verbs

b. **came back**

c. **showed up**

d. **got by**

3. It's raining;_____ the car and I'll drive you to school.

a. **get on**

b. **get in**

c. **get out**

d. **get off**

4. If you_____ for me in the performance, I'll be the one wearing

the giant chicken suit.

a. **look out**

b. **look after**

c. **check out**

d. **check up**

5. _____ to this pole when the subway is moving so you don't fall

down.

a. **Get on**

b. **Catch on**

c. **Stand up**

d. **Hold on**

6. He needs to_____ now; he'll be late for school if he doesn't start

getting ready soon.

a. break up

b. check in

c. get over

d. get up

7. We_____ from Hawaii at seven and landed in Los Angeles just after noon.

a. got off

b. took off

c. wore off

d. ran out

8. When they_____ home, we'll take them to their favorite restaurant.

a. stand up

b. run into

c. come back

d. show up

9. The bus_____ five miles outside of town.

a. broke up

b. broke down

c. fell down

d. fell through

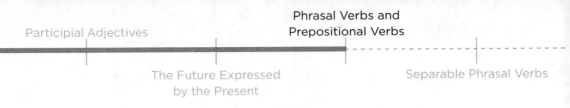

Participial Adjectives

Phrasal Verbs and
Prepositional Verbs

The Future Expressed
by the Present

Separable Phrasal Verbs

10. He was so short he needed a stepping stool to_____ the horse.

  a. get into

  b. get up

  c. get in

  d. get on

ANSWER KEY
1. c; 2. a; 3. b; 4. a; 5. d; 6. d; 7. b; 8. c; 9. b; 10. d

Phrase Builder 2

▶ 14C Phrase Builder 2 (CD 6, Track 7)

call back	
call off	
clean up	
close down	
cut off	
drop off	
figure out	
fill in/out	
fit in	
give up	
hang up	
help with	
let down	
look up	
make up	
pick up	
pull up	

punch in	
put down	
rule out	
sign up	
stand up	
take over	
throw away	
try on	
turn down	
turn in	

✎ Phrase Practice 2

Fill in the blanks with the missing verb or particle for each phrase from Phrase Builder 1 that best complete the sentence.

1. If you find a wallet on the street, you should_____ it in to the police.

2. Don't_____ up too soon when you are trying to do something; you will get better with practice.

3. He said he'd meet me at 7, but it's 9 now and he's still not here. He_____ me up!

4. When you are done having your conversation,_____ up the phone.

5. _____ up your pants; I can see your underwear!

6. He_____ up a story in order to get out of doing his homework.

7. At an ATM, you need to_____ in your PIN number before you can get any money.

Participial Adjectives

Phrasal Verbs and
Prepositional Verbs

The Future Expressed
by the Present

Separable Phrasal Verbs

8. If you don't know the answer, you can_____ it up in the back of the book.

9. Can you_____ me up after work? I don't have a ride.

10. Did you_____ the kids up for soccer lessons? The coach needs their

applications by Friday.

ANSWER KEY
1. turn; 2. give; 3. stood; 4. hang; 5. Pull; 6. made; 7. punch; 8. look; 9. pick; 10. sign

Grammar Builder 2

▶ 14D Grammar Builder 2 (CD 6, Track 8)

SEPARABLE PHRASAL VERBS

As you learned in the last Grammar Builder, some phrasal verbs are inseparable, and some are separable. Separable means that the direct object of the phrasal verb can either follow the entire phrasal verb or come between the main verb and its particle.

Tell him to hang up the phone.	
Tell him to hang the phone up.	
Tell him to hang it up.	

When you replace the direct object with a direct object pronoun, it must always come between the verb and the particle.

Look it up when you get home.	
Call it off.	

Let's look at some more examples of these separable phrasal verbs in use with direct objects and direct object pronouns.

They decided to call off the parade because of rain./They decided to call it off.	

Fill in this form so that we have your information./Fill it in so that we have your information.	
They ruled the athlete out of the competition./They ruled him out of the competition.	
Can you take over the project while I'm on vacation?/Can you take it over while I'm on vacation?	
I've thrown away that old television./I've thrown it away.	

Take It Further
PHRASAL VERBS WITH BACK

When the particle back is used in a phrasal verb, it has the meaning of return. So, if you take something back, you take it to the place where you first got it.

call back Call me back when you get this message.	
give back I'll give this back to you when I'm done with it.	
get back I'll lend this to you, but when will I get it back?	
go back We had to go back to the hotel to change into our evening clothes.	

Participial Adjectives

Phrasal Verbs and
Prepositional Verbs

The Future Expressed
by the Present

Separable Phrasal Verbs

pay back He loaned her twenty dollars and she promised to pay him back next week.	
put back Put this back on the shelf where you got it from.	
take back He should take back what he said to her; it wasn't very nice.	
write back If I write you, will you write me back?	

All of these verbs are separable, except for **come back**, **get back**, and **go back**, which are inseparable and intransitive.

Work Out 2

Rewrite the following sentences by replacing the underlined phrase with a direct object pronoun.

1. Be sure to hang up <u>the phone</u> when you are done talking.

_____

2. He stood <u>his girlfriend</u> up on their date.

_____

3. She will take back <u>the broken cell phone</u> to the store.

_____

4. Pull up your socks.

_____

5. Can I try on this shirt?

_____

6. I'll throw away this old couch.

_____

7. The representative will sign Laura and me up for unlimited texting.

_____

8. I'm trying to figure out the problem.

_____

9. If you fill in this form, we will upgrade your account.

_____

10. They will turn in the money they found.

_____

ANSWER KEY

1. Be sure to hang it up when you are done talking. 2. He stood her up on their date. 3. She will take it back to the store. 4. Pull them up. 5. Can I try it on? 6. I'll throw it away. 7. The representative will sign us up for unlimited texting. 8. I'm trying to figure it out. 9. If you fill it in, we will upgrade your account. 10. They will turn it in.

✎ Drive It Home

Fill in the missing particle in each sentence below.

1. If it's bad, you should take it_____ to the store.

2. We have to get this dog_____ to its owners.

Participial Adjectives

Phrasal Verbs and
Prepositional Verbs

The Future Expressed
by the Present

Separable Phrasal Verbs

3. Can you tell her to call me_____ when she gets home?

4. Go_____ to the restaurant and ask them if they found the umbrella you left there.

5. I promise to pay you_____ for dinner next week.

6. If you don't know a word, you can look it_____ in a dictionary.

7. Stand_____ and let me see how tall you are!

8. Hang_____ the phone!

9. I give_____; how many beans are in the jar?

10. Can you pick_____ a pizza on your way home?

ANSWER KEY
1-5 all back; 6-10 all up

How Did You Do?

Let's see how you did in this lesson. By now, you should:

☐ be able to use phrasal verbs, both separable (hang up) and inseparable (come back) (Still unsure? Jump back to page 216.)

☐ know the meaning of several phrasal verbs with get (Still unsure? Jump back to page 222.)

☐ know the meaning of several phrasal verbs with back (Still unsure? Jump back to page 229.)

✎ Word Recall

Match the phrasal verb below in the left column to its closest meaning in the right column.

1. give back   a. mount

2. throw away   b. disappoint

3. stand up	c. discard
4. show up	d. disqualify
5. rule out	e. return
6. deal with	f. rise
7. let down	g. appear
8. get on	h. handle

ANSWER KEY
1. e; 2. c; 3. f; 4. g; 5. d; 6. h; 7. b; 8. a

Lesson 15: Sentences

In this lesson you'll learn how to:

☐ give advice using should, had better, and ought to

☐ make suggestions using let's

☐ ask for permission using let me, let her, let them, etc.

Sentence Builder 1

▶ 15A Sentence Builder 1 (CD 6, Track 9)

You should go to the dentist before your tooth gets any worse.	
She should see someone about that shooting pain in her arm.	
You'd better come in right away.	
I think I'd better come in sooner.	
You really have to watch out for that!	

Participial Adjectives

Phrasal Verbs and
Prepositional Verbs

The Future Expressed
by the Present

Separable Phrasal Verbs

They have to schedule an appointment before it's too late.	
If she has a chipped tooth, she ought to see a dentist.	
We ought to be more careful.	
The boys are supposed to brush their teeth every night before bed.	
You are supposed to schedule regular cleanings.	
We were supposed to meet at seven.	

✎ Sentence Practice 1

Listen again to Sentence Builder 1 and fill in the missing words below.

1. You_____ to the dentist before your tooth gets any worse.

2. She_____ someone about that shooting pain in her arm.

3. _____ come in right away.

4. I think_____ come in sooner.

5. You really_____ for that!

6. They_____ an appointment before it's too late.

7. If she has a chipped tooth,_____ a dentist.

8. _____ more careful.

9. The boys are_____ their teeth every night before bed.

10. You are_____ regular cleanings.

11. We were_____ at seven.

ANSWER KEY

1. should go; 2. should see; 3. You'd better; 4. I'd better; 5. have to watch out; 6. have to schedule; 7. she ought to see; 8. We ought to be; 9. supposed to brush; 10. supposed to schedule; 11. supposed to meet

Grammar Builder 1

▶ 15B Grammar Builder 1 (CD 6, Track 10)

MORE ON MODALS

In Lesson 9 of Essential English, you learned about modals: words such as can, should, must, need to, want to, and have to. Modals are used to express ability, desire, and obligation.

I need to schedule an appointment with a dentist.	
We can see you this Friday.	
You must brush your teeth every day.	

Modals can also be used to give advice. These modals—should, had better, and ought to—are called "modals of advisability."

Should is used when there are rules or experience which are informing the advice.

You should go to the dentist before your tooth gets any worse.	
We should get inside before it rains.	

Participial Adjectives

Phrasal Verbs and
Prepositional Verbs

The Future Expressed
by the Present

Separable Phrasal Verbs

The negative of should is shouldn't.

She shouldn't bite into that olive; she'll get a cracked tooth.	

Ought to is a more gentle suggestion, but it is advice that the speaker thinks should be taken.

You ought to call my dentist; he's very good at fixing chipped teeth.	
She ought to spend more time reading and less time watching television.	

The negative of ought to is ought to not or ought not to, though these are not used very commonly; shouldn't is usually used instead when negating ought to.

We ought to go to that show; I've been hearing good things about it.	
We shouldn't go to that show; I've been hearing bad things about it.	

Had better is used to suggest that if the advice is not followed, there will be a consequence of harm. It is often followed by or (else) + a clause describing the consequence.

You had better call a dentist or else your tooth could get worse.	
The boys had better behave or they will be in trouble.	

The negative of had better is had better not.

You had better not take the car to work; it needs gas.	

Like the modals mentioned above, **be supposed to** + verb expresses an obligation or an expectation, but also may express doubt over whether or not this will happen.

The boys are supposed to brush their teeth every night before bed.	
We were supposed to meet at 5, but James isn't here yet.	

The negative of **be supposed to** is **be not supposed to**.

She isn't supposed to eat so many sweets.	
I wasn't supposed to be there.	

✎ Work Out 1

Rewrite the sentences below so that the negative sentences are positive and the positive sentences are negative.

1. You shouldn't see a dentist about that tooth.

   _____

2. I was supposed to call him back.

   _____

3. We had better get home before seven.

   _____

4. He ought to eat more sweets.

   _____

Participial Adjectives

Phrasal Verbs and
Prepositional Verbs

The Future Expressed
by the Present

Separable Phrasal Verbs

5. You shouldn't check up on the kids.

_____

6. She had better take over the class.

_____

7. We ought to break up.

_____

8. I had better visit her soon.

_____

9. She is supposed to be here at eight o'clock.

_____

10. He had better not come back home.

_____

ANSWER KEY

1. You should see a dentist about that tooth./You ought to see a dentist about that tooth. 2. I wasn't supposed to call him back. 3. We had better not get home before seven. 4. He ought not to eat more sweets./He shouldn't eat more sweets. 5. You should check up on the kids. 6. She had better not take over the class. 7. We shouldn't break up./We ought not to break up. 8. I had better not visit her soon. 9. She isn't supposed to be here at eight o'clock. 10. He had better come back home.

Sentence Builder 2

▶ 15C Sentence Builder 2 (CD 6, Track 11)

Let's go to the movies tonight.	
Let's call customer service to see if they can help us.	
Let's upgrade to the unlimited texting plan.	

Let's hang up the phone before they answer.	
Let's be honest; this is not a great phone plan.	
Let's not call her back until tomorrow.	
Let me connect you to my supervisor.	
You should let us come into the office today.	
You shouldn't let them behave like that.	
Let her help you with that.	
Let them come back into the room.	
Don't let them run around the store.	

✎ Sentence Practice 2

Listen again to Sentence Builder 2 and fill in the missing words below.

1. _____ to the movies tonight.

2. _____ customer service to see if they can help us out.

3. _____ to the unlimited texting plan.

4. _____ the phone before they answer.

5. _____ ; this is a not a great phone plan.

6. _____ call her back until tomorrow.

7. _____ you to my supervisor.

8. You should_____ into the office today.

9. You shouldn't_____ like that.

10. _____ you with that.

11. _____ into the room.

12. _____ run around the store.

ANSWER KEY

1. Let's go; 2. Let's call; 3. Let's upgrade; 4. Let's hang up; 5. Let's be honest; 6. Let's not; 7. Let me connect; 8. let us come; 9. let them behave; 10. Let her help; 11. Let them come back; 12. Don't let them

Grammar Builder 2

▶ 15D Grammar Builder 2 (CD 6, Track 12)

USING LET

The verb let has various uses in English. When used with an apostrophe s, let's indicates a suggestion, similar to we should.

Let's go to the pool tomorrow.	
Let's watch a movie tonight.	

The negative of let's is let's not.

Let's not forget to call the phone company to ask about our bill.	
Let's not go to that party; I'm so tired.	

The verb let can also be used to ask for permission, meaning allow.

Let her come on the trip with us.	
Let me help you with that.	

Let us bring a side dish to the dinner party.	

The negative of let is don't let.

Don't let them eat all those sweets!	
Don't let me forget to take the trash out tonight.	

Notice the difference between let's and let us. Let's is used for suggestions, while let us is used to ask for permission.

Let's go to the movies. (suggestion)	
Let us go to the movies. (permission)	

Note also that you let someone do something, but you allow someone to do something.

Let me help you with that.	
Allow me to help you with that.	

Let is never used with you, as it is a second person command. (We studied commands in Lesson 1; feel free to go back and review them.)

✎ Work Out 2

A. Write the sentences giving permission to below using let.

1. Allow me to help you with your homework.

_____

2. Allow them to carry those bags for you.

_____

Participial Adjectives

Phrasal Verbs and
Prepositional Verbs

The Future Expressed
by the Present

Separable Phrasal Verbs

3. Don't allow him to eat any more candy.

_____

4. Don't allow me to see what you're working on until it's finished.

_____

5. Allow us to come back to the office to help finish the project.

_____

B. Now make suggestions using let's.

1. look up the answer

_____

2. cook steak for dinner (negative)

_____

3. check into the hotel

_____

4. go to the party (negative)

_____

5. call back the phone company

_____

ANSWER KEY
A. 1. Let me help you with your homework. 2. Let them carry those bags for you. 3. Don't let him eat any more candy. 4. Don't let me see what you're working on until it's finished. 5. Let us come back to the office to help finish the project.
B. 1. Let's look up the answer. 2. Let's not cook steak for dinner. 3. Let's check into the hotel. 4. Let's not go to the party. 5. Let's call back the phone company.

✎ Drive It Home

Make suggestions by filling in the blanks in the sentences below.

1. _____ go see the new Scorsese movie.

2. _____ try on these clothes.

3. _____ not watch that show; it's too scary.

4. _____ be honest; we pay too much for our cell phone plans.

5. _____ cook fish for dinner tonight.

6. _____ check out that new restaurant.

7. _____ not be late to the party.

8. _____ pick up the kids and go to the pool.

9. _____ look it up to see who is correct.

10. _____ not deal with this now.

ANSWER KEY
1-10 all Let's

How Did You Do?

Let's see how you did in this lesson. By now, you should be able to:

☐ give advice using should, had better, and ought to
   (Still unsure? Jump back to page 235.)

☐ make suggestions using let's (Still unsure? Jump back to page 238.)

☐ ask for permission using let me, let her, let them, etc.
   (Still unsure? Jump back to page 240.)

Participial Adjectives

Phrasal Verbs and
Prepositional Verbs

The Future Expressed
by the Present

Separable Phrasal Verbs

✎ Word Recall

Match the modal below in the left column to its best description of its use in the right column.

1. be supposed to	a. advice based on experience or rules
2. can	b. gentle suggestion
3. should	c. desire
4. must	d. obligation
5. had better	e. expectation with possible doubt
6. need to	f. advice with consequences (or else)
7. ought to	g. necessity
8. want to	h. ability

ANSWER KEY
1. e; 2. h; 3. a; 4. d; 5. f; 6. g; 7. b; 8. c

Lesson 16: Conversations

By the end of this lesson, you should be able to:

☐ express an impersonal statement or idea using you, they, and one

☐ use so and such to express cause and effect or to mean very

ⒶⒶ Conversation 1

▶ 16A Conversation 1 (CD 6, Track 13)

Kevin has a problem and needs to see a dentist quickly. Listen in as he calls up his dentist and makes an appointment.

Lorraine: **Davenport Dental, this is Lorraine speaking. Can you please hold for a moment?**

Intermediate English

Kevin:	Um, sure. Yes.
Lorraine:	Thank you. Just one moment please. Don't hang up.
...	
Lorraine:	Thanks for holding on. How can I help you?
Kevin:	My name's Kevin Robinson and I'd like to make an appointment to see a dentist.
Lorraine:	Sure thing, Mr. Robinson. Have you been here before?
Kevin:	Yes, for regular check-ups and cleaning. I was there about eight months or so ago.
Lorraine:	And would you like to schedule another cleaning? I can put you down for, let me pull up the calendar. . .let's see. . . . There's an opening on the 23rd. That's a Tuesday, at 10:15 in the morning.
Kevin:	Oh, no, actually it's not for a cleaning. I think I need to come in sooner.
Lorraine:	Is it an emergency?
Kevin:	Well, I'm not sure if it's an emergency. But I have a chipped tooth. Or maybe even a cracked tooth.
Lorraine:	A chipped tooth?
Kevin:	I think it's cracked, actually.
Lorraine:	What happened?
Kevin:	I was eating a salad, and . . .
Lorraine:	Let me guess. You bit into an olive pit?
Kevin:	Yes! How did you guess?
Lorraine:	We come across that a lot. You really have to watch out for olives! Even if they say they're pitted, it's really easy to run into one that still has a pit. Olive pits are such a common cause of chipped or cracked teeth.
Kevin:	Well, that's what I did. I bit down on it, heard a really weird cracking sound, and then there was a shooting pain coming from my back tooth.
Lorraine:	What happens when you touch the tooth?
Kevin:	It's really painful! I've never felt such a pain in my tooth!

Participial Adjectives

Phrasal Verbs and
Prepositional Verbs

The Future Expressed
by the Present

Separable Phrasal Verbs

Lorraine:	Yes, you'd better come in right away. It sounds like it's cracked, not just chipped. But as soon as you get here, the dentist will take a look, and he'll let you know whether it's cracked or not. You ought to get here as soon as possible. We'll fit you in.
Kevin:	I can make it there this afternoon. I really appreciate your seeing me so quickly.
Lorraine:	Of course. You'd better stay away from hot or cold drinks before then.
Kevin:	Don't worry! I don't plan on eating or drinking anything until I see the dentist.

✎ Conversation Practice 1

Answer the following questions based on the dialogue.

1. Has Kevin been to Davenport Dental before? Why?

_____

2. When was the last time he was there?

_____

3. When does Lorraine say she can schedule him for a cleaning?

_____

4. Why does Kevin need an appointment, not a cleaning?

_____

5. How did Kevin hurt his tooth?

_____

6. What sound did Kevin hear when he bit down on the olive?

_____

7. What kind of pain was there when he bit down on the olive?

_____

8. What happens when Kevin touches his tooth?

_____

9. Does Lorraine think his tooth is chipped or cracked?

_____

10. What does Lorraine tell Kevin he'd better stay away from before he sees the

dentist?

_____

ANSWER KEY

1. Yes, for regular check-ups and cleanings. 2. He was there about eight months ago. 3. She can put him down for Tuesday the 23rd, at 10:15 in the morning. 4. He has a chipped tooth, or maybe a cracked tooth. 5. He bit into an olive pit. 6. He heard a really weird cracking sound. 7. There was a shooting pain. 8. It's really painful. 9. Lorraine thinks his tooth is cracked. 10. He'd better stay away from hot or cold drinks.

Grammar Builder 1

▷ 16B Grammar Builder 1 (CD 6, Track 14)

IMPERSONAL EXPRESSIONS WITH YOU, THEY, AND ONE

The pronouns you, they, and one are used when the specific subject of a sentence is unclear, to talk about people in general, or to express a general thought or idea. You and one are used to talk about any person or people in general.

You can really get hurt riding motorcycles.	
One might try switching to sugar free drinks to avoid cavities.	

Participial Adjectives

Phrasal Verbs and
Prepositional Verbs

The Future Expressed
by the Present

Separable Phrasal Verbs

They are interchangeable, but **one** is more formal.

You can never tell if what they're saying is true.	
One never can tell if what they're saying is true.	
How do you translate this sentence?	
How does one translate this sentence?	

They is used to talk about some person or some people, where the people might not be clearly defined.

Even if they say it's pitted, sometimes there are still pits.	
They make the best salad at this restaurant.	

They can be used in casual English if you don't want to or are unable to identify a specific person, or if the gender of the person is unclear.

Did you see the person who stole your car? Yes, they were wearing a red jacket.	
The person with the best presentation will be rewarded; they will win a cash prize.	

They is often used with **say** to express a popularly believed fact or popular saying.

They say you shouldn't brush your teeth too hard.	
They say it's always calmest before a storm.	

✎ Work Out 1

Fill in the blanks below with an impersonal you, one, or they to complete each sentence. (Pay attention to the clues in parentheses.)

1. _____ make a great dessert at this restaurant.

2. _____ have to be careful driving when it's snowing outside.

3. _____ ought to be on time to an appointment. (formal)

4. Even if_____ said that you should be there at ten, you should go early.

5. Did you see what the person was wearing?_____ had on a blue hat.

6. How do_____ get wine out of the carpet?

7. _____ should be sure to close the door when entering the room. (formal)

8. _____ never know what might happen.

9. _____ say these things take time.

10. Did you call the hotel? Yes;_____ don't have any rooms left.

ANSWER KEY
1. They; 2. You; 3. One; 4. they; 5. They; 6. you; 7. One; 8. You; 9. They; 10. they

ⒸⒸ Conversation 2

▶ 16C Conversation 2 (CD 6, Track 15)

Andrea has upgraded her cell phone service, and she has a question about her bill. Listen carefully as she makes her way through the automated customer service line.

Automated
Operator: Welcome to Gateway Cellular Communications. Listen
                carefully, as our menu options have changed.

Participial Adjectives

Phrasal Verbs and
Prepositional Verbs

The Future Expressed
by the Present

Separable Phrasal Verbs

Andrea: So typical ... Every time I call, their menu options have changed. But they always seem the same to me!

Automated Operator: If you're a new customer and would like to find out more about Gateway Cellular Communications products, press one now. If you're a business owner and would like to hear how Gateway can help your business needs, press two.

Andrea: Come on. Move along now. They always waste your time before you're able to actually speak to a person!

Automated Operator: If you're an existing customer and would like to speak with someone on our technical support team, press three. If you're an existing customer and have a question about your bill, press four.

Andrea: Ah, there we go. That sounds right. Pressing four now ...

Automated Operator: Please wait while I put you through to the right department. Please do not hang up. Your call is very important to us.

Andrea: Yeah, yeah, yeah, I'm such a cherished customer ...

Automated Operator: So that we can better serve you, please enter your ten-digit phone number, starting with the area code.

Andrea: Let's see ... Six Four Six ... and the rest.

Automated Operator: Thank you. Please continue to hold, and your call will be taken in the order in which it was received.

...

Simon: Good afternoon, Gateway Billing. This is Simon. I see that you've punched in your phone number. Can I get your billing zip code?

Andrea: One Two Oh Seven Five.

Simon: Thank you. And who am I speaking with today, please?

Andrea:	Andrea Martin.
Simon:	Thank you, Ms. Martin. And for verification, can you tell me your four-digit pin?
Andrea:	One Two Three Four.
Simon:	That's correct. But we do recommend that customers choose a unique pin. One Two Three Four is such a common pin.
Andrea:	I know, I ought to change it, but it's so easy to remember, and you have so many different pins and passwords to remember now.
Simon:	I understand, ma'am. What can I help you with today?
Andrea:	Well, I just got my first bill. I signed up for an unlimited voice and data plan, which I thought was ninety-nine dollars.
Simon:	That's right. Plus any applied fees.
Andrea:	Right. But there's a charge for forty dollars that I don't understand.
Simon:	Okay, I've pulled up your account, and I can see that you've just activated your service.
Andrea:	Well, I upgraded my service last month. I didn't activate my service.
Simon:	Right. There's a forty dollar one-time activation fee.
Andrea:	An activation fee? But this isn't a newly activated account. It's a recently upgraded account. They didn't tell me anything about an activation fee.
Simon:	I understand, ma'am. Let me transfer you to the Billing Dispute Resolution Department.
Andrea:	But ...
Automated Operator:	Please hold while I transfer your call. Please do not hang up. Your call is very important to us.
Andrea:	So typical! They trap you in these automated customer service loops and hope you'll go away before you speak to anyone!

Participial Adjectives

Phrasal Verbs and
Prepositional Verbs

The Future Expressed
by the Present

Separable Phrasal Verbs

✎ Conversation Practice 2

Answer the following questions based on the dialogue.

1. What has changed according to the automated operator?

_____

2. What number should Andrea press if she's a new customer?

_____

3. Why does Andrea press four?

_____

4. What is the first thing Simon asks Andrea for?

_____

5. What is wrong with Andreas PIN?

_____

6. Why does Andrea have "1234" as her PIN?

_____

7. How much does an unlimited voice and data plan cost?

_____

8. Why is there a charge on Andrea's bill for forty dollars?

_____

9. Is Andrea's account a newly activated account?

_____

10. What department does Simon transfer Andrea to?

_____

ANSWER KEY

1. Their menu options have changed. 2. She should press one. 3. Because she's an existing customer with questions about her bill. 4. He asks her for her zip code. 5. It is too common; they recommend that customers choose a unique PIN. 6. Because it is so easy to remember. 7. It costs ninety dollars. 8. It is a one-time activation fee. 9. No, it is a recently upgraded account. 10. He transfers her to the Billing Dispute Resolution Department.

Grammar Builder 2

▶ 16D Grammar Builder 2 (CD 6, Track 16)

SO **AND** SUCH

In Lesson 7 you saw how **so** can be used as a coordinating conjunction.

Let us know what your problem is, so (that) we can direct your call.	

This meaning is similar to **in order to** which you saw in Lesson 6.

So can also be used with **that** to describe cause and effect. When connecting two clauses, it is placed before the adjective or adverb in the clause describing the cause, and **that** (unless it is omitted in spoken English) comes before the effect clause.

They were nice on the phone. I signed up for another year of service. They were <u>so</u> nice on the phone (that) I signed up for another year of service.	
The soup was hot. I couldn't eat it. The soup was <u>so</u> hot (that) I couldn't eat it.	

Participial Adjectives

Phrasal Verbs and
Prepositional Verbs

The Future Expressed
by the Present

Separable Phrasal Verbs

Notice how the following two sentences mean the same thing, but the word order changes:

It was a bad toothache, <u>so</u> I called the dentist.	
The toothache was <u>so</u> bad that I called the dentist.	

So ... that is also used with **much, many, little,** and **few.**

We had <u>so little</u> work to do that they sent us home early.	
<u>So many</u> people signed up for the new service that they had to expand the business.	

So is also used with adverbs.

She read the options <u>so quickly</u> that I couldn't hear them.	
They did <u>so badly</u> that the teacher had to fail them.	

Such ... that can also be used to express the same cause and effect by surrounding a modified noun (adjective + noun).

It was good service. We decided to switch plans. It was <u>such</u> good service (<u>that</u>) we decided to switch plans.	
There was a bad pain in my tooth. I decided to call the dentist. There was <u>such</u> a bad pain in my tooth (<u>that</u>) I decided to call the dentist.	

So is never used with a modified noun that doesn't contain an indefinite article (**a, an**). When **so ... that** is used with a modified noun, the article and adjective switch places. Note the word order below.

It was <u>such a good experience</u> that I told all of my friends.	
It was <u>so good an experience</u> that I told all of my friends.	

Such and **so** are used casually without an effect clause to mean **very**.

That's <u>so</u> typical.	
She's <u>such a difficult person.	
It's <u>so</u> easy to remember!	

✎ Work Out 2

Rewrite the sentences below to create cause and effect using **so ... that** and **such ... that**.

1. She was put on hold for a long time. She hung up the phone.

   _____

2. They hung up quickly. I couldn't ask them my question.

   _____

3. Their service is good. I recommended them to friends.

   _____

4. His tooth hurt badly. He called the dentist.

   _____

Participial Adjectives

Phrasal Verbs and
Prepositional Verbs

The Future Expressed
by the Present

Separable Phrasal Verbs

5. He had a bad toothache. He called the dentist.

_____

6. There were many people. We couldn't get a reservation.

_____

7. It was a nice day out. We went for a walk.

_____

8. I had a great time. I will visit again.

_____

9. We are tired. We're going to bed.

_____

10. There was little time. We didn't see the dentist.

_____

ANSWER KEY

1. She was put on hold for such a long time that she hung up the phone./She was put on hold for so long a time that she hung up the phone. 2. They hung up so quickly that I couldn't ask them my question. 3. Their service is so good that I recommended them to friends. 4. His tooth hurt so badly that he called the dentist. 5. He had such a bad toothache that he called the dentist./He had so bad a toothache that he called the dentist. 6. There were so many people that we couldn't get a reservation. 7. It was such a nice day out that we went for a walk./It was so nice a day out that we went for a walk. 8. I had such a great time that I will visit again./I had so great a time that I will visit again. 9. We are so tired that we're going to bed. 10. There was so little time that we didn't see the dentist.

✎ Drive It Home

Fill in the blanks below with **so** or **such**.

1. She's_____ difficult!

2. There's_____ little to eat in the house.

3. This is_____ easy.

4. We're going to be_____ late.

5. Customer service was_____ helpful.

6. This is_____ a fancy restaurant.

7. These are_____ good deals.

8. They are_____ nice people.

9. We had_____ a great time.

10. They provide_____ helpful information!

ANSWER KEY
1-5 all so; 6-10 all such

⊕ Culture Note
CUSTOMER SERVICE

Most Americans have to deal with Customer Service on a regular basis. Whether you are trying to activate your phone, upgrade your account, or switch your plan, you might at some point have to speak to a Customer Service representative to help you deal with your account. Even if you aren't dealing with a telephone company, most companies have a Customer Service department to help their customers solve issues and get through problems with their products.

The experience can be so frustrating, but many companies are working to make the experience more positive by encouraging their employees to be as courteous and helpful as possible. There are so many different ways to handle customers, that these companies often change their procedure, and this is why when you call a Customer Service line, you might hear those dreaded words: *Listen carefully, as our menu options have changed ...*

How Did You Do?

Let's see how you did in this lesson. By now, you should be able to:

☐ express an impersonal statement or idea using **you**, **they**, and **one** (Still unsure? Jump back to page 247.)

☐ use **so** and **such** to express cause and effect or to mean **very** (Still unsure? Jump back to page 253.)

Word Recall

Let's review some phrasal verbs you learned in this unit. Match the words in the left column below to their best definition in the right column.

1. come back	a. forfeit
2. go away	b. drop
3. put down	c. leave
4. give up	d. examine
5. fit in	e. deliver
6. check up	f. accommodate
7. cut off	g. return
8. drop off	h. disconnect

ANSWER KEY
1. g; 2. c; 3. b; 4. a; 5. f; 6. d; 7. h; 8. e

Don't forget to practice and reinforce what you've learned by visiting **www.livinglanguage.com/languagelab** for flashcards, games, and quizzes!

Unit 4 Quiz

Let's put the most essential English words and grammar points you've learned so far to practice in a few exercises. It's important to be sure that you've mastered this material before you move on. Score yourself at the end of the review and see if you need to go back for more practice, or if you're ready to move on to Unit 5.

A. Choose the correct participial adjective to complete the sentence.

1. I felt a (**shooting/shot**) pain in my left arm.

2. The (**damaging/damaged**) houses had to be rebuilt.

B. Choose the correct tense of the verb in parentheses to complete each sentence.

1. As soon as we_____, we will call the babysitter. (**leave**)

2. She will call you when she_____ home. (**get**)

C. Fill in the missing particle in each sentence.

1. We ran_____ our friend Sam at the grocery store.

2. Get_____the car and I'll drive you to the station.

3. When they enter the room, stand_____ to show respect.

D. Rewrite the sentences below replacing the underlined noun with a direct object pronoun.

1. Look up the number of the restaurant so we can call them.

   _____

2. Hang up the phone when you are done talking.

   _____

3. Pick up your sister after tennis practice.

   _____

E. Choose the best modal to complete the sentence.

1. They_____ go to the dentist or that tooth could get worse.

2. _____ we leave soon?

3. They_____ to brush their teeth every night before bed.

F. Fill in the blank with **let us** or **let's** based on the clue in parentheses.

1. _____ visit our grandparents this weekend. (suggestion)

2. _____ visit our grandparents this weekend. (permission)

G. Fill in the blank with the appropriate impersonal pronoun.

1. _____ can get hurt playing rough like that.

2. _____ say that it takes a while to learn English.

H. Combine the following sentences into one sentence using **so** and **such**. Give both options in your answer where possible. (Use **that** in your answers.)

1. It was a good show. We decided to see it again.

   _____

2. They were kind to her. She recommended them to others.

   _____

3. It was stormy weather. They had to go inside.

   _____

ANSWER KEY
A. 1. shooting; 2. damaged
B. 1. leave; 2. gets
C. 1. into; 2. in; 3. up
D. 1. Look it up so we can call them. 2. Hang it up when you are done talking. 3. Pick her up after tennis practice.
E. 1. had better; 2. Should; 3. ought/are supposed
F. 1. Let's; 2. Let us
G. 1. You/One; 2. They
H. 1. It was such a good show that we decided to see it again./It was so good a show that we decided to see it again. 2. They were so kind to her that she recommended them to others. 3. It was such stormy weather that they had to go inside.

How Did You Do?

Give yourself a point for every correct answer, then use the following key to tell whether you're ready to move on:

0–7 points: It's probably a good idea to go back through the lesson again. You may be moving too quickly, or there may be too much "down time" between your contact with English. Remember that it's better to spend 30 minutes with English three or four times a week than it is to spend two or three hours just once a week. Find a pace that's comfortable for you, and spread your contact hours out as much as you can.

8–12 points: You would benefit from a review before moving on. Go back and spend a little more time on the specific points that gave you trouble. Re-read the Grammar Builder sections that were difficult, and do the work out one more time. Don't forget about the online supplemental practice material, either. Go to **www.livinglanguage.com/languagelab** for games and quizzes that will reinforce the material from this unit.

13–17 points: Good job! There are just a few points that you could consider reviewing before moving on. If you haven't worked with the games and quizzes on **www.livinglanguage.com/languagelab**, please give them a try.

18–20 points: Great! You're ready to move on to the next unit.

 **points**

Unit 5:
Taking a Trip

In this unit, you'll learn how to talk about going on a trip. You'll learn new vocabulary related to vacation and road travel and how to talk about ongoing events in the future. You'll also learn more complex grammar like how to use adjectives and verbs followed by specific prepositions, form gerunds as nouns and use gerunds with verbs. Finally, you'll learn how to distinguish the verb pairs **raise/rise, sit/set, lie/lay**.

Let's get started!

Lesson 17: Words

In this lesson you'll learn:

☐ vocabulary for talking about road travel

☐ vocabulary related to staying in a hotel

☐ how to talk about ongoing events in the future using the future progressive

☐ how to use adjectives followed by certain prepositions

Adjectives Followed
by Prepositions

Verbs Followed by
Gerunds

Word Builder 1

▶ 17A Word Builder 1 (CD 6, Track 17)

road, highway, freeway, street, lane, avenue, alley, gravel road, dirt road	
exit, exit ramp, entrance ramp, passing lane, dotted line	
traffic, traffic jam, accident, construction, lane closed, detour, rush hour	
GPS, map, road atlas, mile marker, sign, route	
miles, yards, miles per hour (MPH)	
scenery, countryside, farmland, industrial area, scenic route, villages	
road trip, rest stop, pit stop, rest area, gas station	
steering wheel, gas pedal, brakes, windshield, mirrors, windshield wipers, windows, headlights, blinkers	
drive, accelerate, decelerate, stop, brake, slam on the brakes, slow down, speed up	
pass, veer, swerve, steer	
vacation, hotel, beach, skiing, cabin, lake	
relax, enjoy, unwind, disconnect	
stretch your legs, keep an eye out	

Infinitives

Verbs Followed by
Prepositions

Verbs Followed by
Infinitives

Verbs Followed by an Object
and an Infinitive

✎ Word Practice 1

Fill in the blanks in each sentence below with the best word from Word Practice 1.

1. When a road is closed because of construction, you have to take

   a_____, or a route around the construction.

2. A_____ is a public place at the side of the highway with

   parking, restrooms, and vending machines for when drivers need to stop.

3. To drive faster, you_____ by stepping on the gas pedal.

4. When it rains, you should turn on your_____

   _____ so that you can see through the windshield.

5. To get off the highway, you will take the_____.

6. While driving across America, you can take the_____

   to see some beautiful scenery.

7. They are taking a_____ to Utah to go skiing.

8. You should only_____ other cars in a passing lane or when there is a dotted

   line.

9. It took them hours to get to the city because of horrible_____ at

   rush hour.

10. If you are tired from driving, you should stop at a rest stop to_____

    _____.

ANSWER KEY
1. **detour**; 2. **rest area**; 3. **accelerate**; 4. **windshield wipers**; 5. **exit ramp**; 6. **scenic route**; 7. **vacation**;
8. **pass**; 9. **traffic**; 10. **stretch your legs**

Grammar Builder 1

▶ 17B Grammar Builder 1 (CD 6, Track 18)

THE FUTURE PROGRESSIVE

You learned the present and past progressive in previous lessons; now let's look at the future progressive. The future progressive is formed with **will be** + the **–ing** form of a verb.

We will be going on vacation this August.	
Will you be taking a train to get there?	

There is another form of the future progressive expressed with **be going to be** + the **–ing** form of the verb. It is usually used to express actions happening in the near future.

He is going to be working on this project all afternoon.	
We'll be taking the next exit.	

Both forms of the future progressive express the same thing: an action that begins in the future and continues for a period of time further into the future. Use the future progressive to emphasize that an action will occur over a period of time, instead of just a one-time action in the future.

They'll be driving for hours.	
We'll be staying in this hotel all week.	

You can also use the future progressive to express a future action that will be interrupted by another future action.

The train will be departing when we get to the station.	
Will you be driving to the cabin when we arrive?	

Note that the interrupting action is expressed with the simple present, but indicates the future.

The future progressive can also be used to express intent or plans, similarly to the simple future.

I'm going to be traveling through the Alps next week.	
She's going to be visiting her parents next week.	

Keep in mind the word order when the future progressive is in the form of a question: the helping verb comes before the pronoun.

Will you be traveling by car?	
Are you going to be traveling by car?	

✎ Work Out 1

Change the sentences below to the future progressive.

1. We drive to the Catskills.

_____

Adjectives Followed
by Prepositions

Verbs Followed by
Gerunds

2. She takes a class on Fridays.

_____

3. They are visiting their children.

_____

4. I saw a doctor.

_____

5. He goes on vacation in the Caribbean.

_____

6. Will you stay in a hotel?

_____

7. We are having steak for dinner.

_____

8. He took the train to Denver.

_____

9. They watch this movie all night.

_____

10. I brought a salad to potluck.

_____

ANSWER KEY
1. **We will be driving to the Catskills./We are going to be driving to the Catskills. 2. She will be taking a class on Fridays./She is going to be taking a class on Fridays. 3. They will be visiting their children./They are going to be visiting their children. 4. I will be seeing a doctor./I am going to**

Infinitives

Verbs Followed by
Prepositions

Verbs Followed by
Infinitives

Verbs Followed by an Object
and an Infinitive

be seeing a doctor. 5. He will be going on vacation in the Caribbean./He is going to be going on vacation in the Caribbean. 6. Will you be staying in a hotel?/Are you going to be staying in a hotel? 7. We will be having steak for dinner./We are going to be having steak for dinner. 8. He will be taking the train to Denver./He is going to be taking the train to Denver. 9. They will be watching this movie all night./They are going to be watching this movie all night. 10. I will be bringing a salad to potluck./I am going to be bringing a salad to potluck.

Word Builder 2

▶ 17C Word Builder 2 (CD 6, Track 19)

hotel, resort, hotel room, double, single, suite, balcony, view, ocean view, garden view	
pool, indoor pool, outdoor pool, whirlpool, hot tub	
room service, continental breakfast, complimentary breakfast, restaurant, bar	
amenities, gym, workout room, business center, conference room, fax machine, scanner, Wi-Fi	
modern, convenient, comfortable, all-inclusive	
stay, reserve, book, check in, check out	
renovate, remodel, update	
concierge, porter, bellhop, front desk clerk, hotel manager, resort director	
key card, laundry bag, mini-bar	

✎ Word Practice 2

Fill in the blanks in each sentence below with the best word from Word Practice 1.

1. When you _____ a place, you are rebuilding or redesigning it to make it more modern.

2. If you don't know where to go for dinner, you can ask the _____ at the hotel, or the front desk clerk.

3. People who do a lot of work on their computers like to stay in a hotel that provides free _____.

4. When you don't want to leave your room for breakfast, you can order _____.

5. It's nice to stay at a hotel with an _____ so that you can go swimming even if it's cold out.

6. You need a _____ in order to get into most hotel rooms.

7. If your bed isn't _____, you probably won't sleep very well.

8. When you need to print something, you can visit a hotel's

   _____.

9. Hotels often provide a gym or _____ for guests to exercise in.

10. A resort will often be _____, meaning the room, meals, and drinks are part of the price.

ANSWER KEY

1. renovate; 2. concierge; 3. Wi-Fi; 4. room service; 5. indoor pool; 6. key card; 7. comfortable; 8. business center; 9. workout room; 10. all-inclusive

Infinitives

Verbs Followed by
Prepositions

Verbs Followed by
Infinitives

Verbs Followed by an Object
and an Infinitive

Grammar Builder 2

▶ 17D Grammar Builder 2 (CD 6, Track 20)

ADJECTIVES FOLLOWED BY PREPOSITIONS

Some adjectives in English are followed by certain prepositions before an object. It may be logical, but not always. Most of these adjective and preposition pairs will have to be memorized.

accused of	
afraid of	
amazed at	
angry at/with	
bored by/with	
capable of	
concerned about	
devoted to	
disappointed in/with	
disgusted by	
divorced from	
equipped with	
excited about/for	
exhausted from	
familiar with	
frightened at/by	
impressed by/with	
interested in	
jealous of	
known for	

Adjectives Followed
by Prepositions

made of	
married to	
nervous about	
pleased with	
polite to	
prepared for	
proud of	
qualified for	
related to	
responsible for	
saddened by	
satisfied with	
sorry for/about	
tired of	
upset with	
worried about	

You can find a more complete list of adjectives and their corresponding prepositions in the grammar summary. Here are some example sentences.

I'm tired of riding in the car.	
We think you'll be pleased with the view.	
They were sorry for canceling our reservation.	
She wasn't prepared for the rain.	
Were you impressed with their service?	
You won't be disappointed in the food at our restaurant.	

Infinitives

Verbs Followed by
Prepositions

Verbs Followed by
Infinitives

Verbs Followed by an Object
and an Infinitive

✎ Work Out 2

Choose the best preposition to complete each sentence below.

1. Are you afraid_____ the dark?

   a. by

   b. of

   c. for

   d. with

2. Who is responsible_____ writing the report?

   a. with

   b. for

   c. in

   d. by

3. You must be proud_____ your daughter!

   a. by

   b. of

   c. with

   d. in

4. This restaurant is known_____ its key lime pie.

   a. for

   b. about

   c. by

   d. of

Adjectives Followed
by Prepositions

Verbs Followed by
Gerunds

5. He is obviously jealous_____ her.

   a. with

   b. in

   c. for

   d. of

6. We are getting excited_____ our trip to Mallorca!

   a. to

   b. about

   c. of

   d. in

7. Are you familiar_____ this part of town?

   a. in

   b. of

   c. with

   d. to

8. Would you be interested_____ hearing more about our hotel?

   a. of

   b. with

   c. in

   d. to

9. Each room is equipped_____ a mini-bar and a coffee machine.

   a. with

   b. to

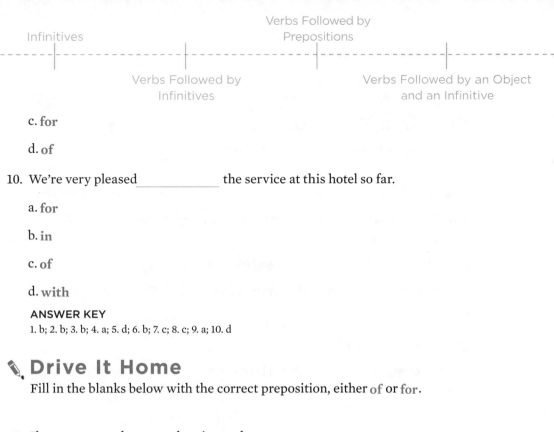

c. **for**

d. **of**

10. We're very pleased_____ the service at this hotel so far.

a. **for**

b. **in**

c. **of**

d. **with**

ANSWER KEY

1. b; 2. b; 3. b; 4. a; 5. d; 6. b; 7. c; 8. c; 9. a; 10. d

✎ Drive It Home

Fill in the blanks below with the correct preposition, either **of** or **for**.

1. She was accused_____ cheating on her exam.

2. What are you so afraid_____ ?

3. I was jealous_____ her dress.

4. They were so proud_____ their daughters.

5. I'm tired_____ driving.

6. We are very excited_____ our vacation.

7. He is known_____ being late to events.

8. Are you prepared_____ the presentation?

9. Is he qualified_____ this position?

10. We are sorry_____ your loss.

ANSWER KEY

1-5 all **of**; 6-10 all **for**

How Did You Do?

Let's see how you did in this lesson. By now, you should know:

☐ vocabulary for talking about road travel (Still unsure? Jump back to page 264.)

☐ how to talk about ongoing events in the future using the future progressive (Still unsure? Jump back to page 266.)

☐ vocabulary related to staying in a hotel (Still unsure? Jump back to page 269.)

☐ how to use adjectives followed by certain prepositions (Still unsure? Jump back to page 271.)

✎ Word Recall

Match each word in the left column below with its best match in the right column.

1. scenery	a. continental breakfast
2. construction	b. map
3. decelerate	c. workout room
4. hotel	d. view
5. road atlas	e. resort
6. room service	f. detour
7. gym	g. brake
8. renovate	h. remodel

ANSWER KEY
1. d; 2. f; 3. g; 4. e; 5. b; 6. a; 7. c; 8. h

Lesson 18: Phrases

In this lesson you'll learn how to:

☐ form and use gerunds as nouns

☐ use gerunds with verbs

☐ use possessors to modify gerunds

Phrase Builder 1

▶ 18A Phrase Builder 1 (CD 6, Track 21)

tired of sitting	
looking out the window	
seeing the sights	
driving through an area	
standing around a field	
complaining about the drive	
listening to music	
dreaming of wonderful things	
arriving at the hotel	
checking out of the hotel	
lying in the sun	
being on vacation	
stretching your legs	
drive without stopping	
go skiing	
go swimming	

✎ Phrase Practice 1

Fill in the blanks below with the best phrase from Phrase Builder 1.

1. I like_____ on the radio.

2. _____ can be nice, but be sure to wear

   sunscreen!

3. _____ isn't always easy for people who love

   to work.

4. When you_____, you can get

   tired of being in the car.

5. Stop_____; we

   still have three hours to go before we get there.

6. You should think about_____;

   we've been sitting in this car for too long.

7. _____ is easier when

   you've already paid the bill.

8. Do you want to_____ in the mountains this winter?

9. They got tired of_____ around the city and

   decided to go back to the hotel.

10. I'm so_____ in this car. Can we make a pit stop?

    ANSWER KEY

    1. listening to music; 2. Lying in the sun; 3. Being on vacation; 4. drive without stopping; 5.
    complaining about the drive; 6. stretching your legs; 7. Checking out of the hotel; 8. go skiing; 9.
    seeing the sights; 10. tired of sitting

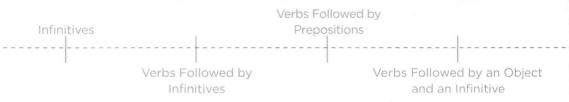
Grammar Builder 1

▶ 18B Grammar Builder 1 (CD 6, Track 22)

GERUNDS

Gerunds are the –ing form of a verb, such as taking or driving, acting as a noun. Since it acts as the noun in a sentence, it will behave the same as a noun and appear as either the subject or object of a verb or preposition. Gerunds can be the subject of a sentence.

Driving is fun.	
Smoking is not allowed aboard the aircraft.	

Gerunds can be the object of a verb.

She doesn't like driving.	
Our friend loves cooking.	
She thinks hiking is boring.	

Gerunds can also be the object of a preposition.

We talked about traveling to Africa.	
I'm excited about being on vacation!	
Are you thinking of going to the beach?	

You can negate a gerund by placing not in front of it.

You should try not drinking for a week.	
The thought of not working makes me nervous.	
Not seeing the sign is not an excuse to speed.	

Pay attention to the fact that the gerund looks the same as the –ing form of the verb, but it acts differently. In the sentence **we are thinking about going to the pool today** for example, **thinking** is the present participle, while **going** is the gerund.

Take It Further
GO + GERUND

The verb **go** can be combined with a gerund to express an activity, usually a leisure activity.

go swimming **We like to go swimming in the summer.**	
go fishing **He is going to go fishing this weekend.**	
go hiking **They go hiking in the Catskills every autumn.**	
go dancing **Let's go dancing!**	
go shopping **She and I are going shopping after work.**	

✎ Work Out 1

In each sentence below, underline or circle the gerund.

1. You should try not doing that.

   _____

2. Seeing you again is making me happy.

   _____

3. They are thinking about going on vacation in August.

   _____

4. When are we going to stop driving? I need to stretch my legs.

   _____

5. Once we finish eating, we are going to watch a movie.

   _____

6. I was asking the professor about writing my paper.

   _____

7. Discussing this topic is exciting to me.

   _____

8. She said she was sorry for taking his book.

   _____

9. By not telling him that they were coming first, they gave him a big surprise.

   _____

10. We recommend visiting the Louvre while you are traveling to Paris.

    _____

ANSWER KEY
1. not doing; 2. Seeing; 3. going; 4. driving; 5. eating; 6. writing; 7. discussing; 8. taking; 9. not telling; 10. visiting

Phrase Builder 2

▶ 18C Word Builder 2 (CD 6, Track 23)

advise being cautious	
anticipate missing the class	
avoid braking too hard	
consider writing a letter	
delay paying the bills	
deny breaking the window	
discuss taking a vacation	
dislike lying in the sun	
enjoy reading a book	
finish eating	
can't help being jealous	
keep talking	
mind holding on to this	
miss seeing my family	
postpone taking a trip	
practice dancing	
quit smoking	
recall seeing that man	
recommend visiting that museum	
regret saying those things	
resent being in this position	
resist taking a bite	
risk missing our flight	

Infinitives	Verbs Followed by Prepositions	
	Verbs Followed by Infinitives	Verbs Followed by an Object and an Infinitive
stop making mistakes		
suggest taking the scenic route		
tolerate misbehaving		
understand having to take a vacation		

✎ Word Practice 2

Fill in the blanks below with the best phrase from Phrase Builder 2 to complete each sentence.

1. You should really_____; cigarettes are bad for

   your health.

2. When you're in New York, I_____

   _____ to see its collection of tribal art.

3. When you_____ your dinner, you can have dessert.

4. It's been so long since I've been home; I_____.

5. We_____ until we have enough

   money in our account.

6. If the car in front of you stops suddenly, you should_____

   _____ or else you might veer off the road.

7. They_____, so they never

   take a beach vacation.

8. We had to_____ because all of

   the airlines were on strike.

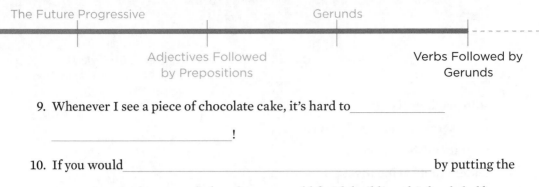
9. Whenever I see a piece of chocolate cake, it's hard to_____

_____!

10. If you would_____ by putting the

wrong pegs in the wrong holes, then we could finish building this bookshelf!

ANSWER KEY
1. quit smoking; 2. recommend visiting that museum; 3. finish eating; 4. miss seeing my family; 5. delay paying the bills; 6 avoid braking too hard; 7. dislike lying in the sun; 8. postpone taking a trip; 9. resist taking a bite; 10. stop making mistakes

Grammar Builder 2

▶ 18D Grammar Builder 2 (CD 6, Track 24)

VERBS FOLLOWED BY GERUNDS

There are certain verbs that must be followed by gerunds (instead of the infinitive, which you'll learn in the next lesson).

avoid You should avoid taking that road late at night.	
finish Finish eating your dinner and then we will watch a movie.	
keep If you keep talking during class, the teacher will be mad.	
mind Would you mind holding this for me?	
miss I missed seeing him when he was in town.	

stop	
Stop kicking the back of my seat!	

Some other common verbs that must be followed by gerunds are: admit, advise, anticipate, consider, delay, deny, discuss, dislike, enjoy, can't help, postpone, practice, quit, recall, recommend, regret, resent, resist, risk, suggest, tolerate, and understand.

There are some verbs that can be followed by either a gerund or an infinitive; we'll look at those in the next lesson after we study infinitives.

Take It Further
GERUNDS USED WITH POSSESSIVES

Gerunds can also be modified by a possessor. In formal English, the possessive adjective is used.

They worried about <u>my</u> driving home so late at night.	
He didn't like <u>our</u> taking the book without asking.	

In informal English, the direct object pronoun is used.

They worried about <u>me</u> driving home so late at night.	
He didn't like <u>us</u> taking the book without asking.	

Similarly, when using a proper noun, the possessive is used in formal English, while the proper noun as a direct object is used in casual English.

He was unhappy with **Joan's arriving** late to dinner. (formal)	
He was unhappy with **Joan arriving** late to dinner. (informal)	

✎ Work Out 2

Fill in the blanks below with the verb in parentheses in its correct form.

You may have to change the spelling of some verbs to form the gerund.

1. If you keep_____ late to things, one day we're going to miss a plane. (**be**)

2. Make sure the kids practice_____ piano before they go out with their friends. (**play**)

3. They suggested_____ an appointment if I wanted to see the doctor this week. (**make**)

4. Some people really enjoy_____ in the shower. (**sing**)

5. We miss_____ out for dinner. (**go**)

6. I couldn't resist_____ her where she got her dress. (**ask**)

7. She dislikes_____ long distances. (**drive**)

8. He can't help_____ whatever comes to the top of his head. (**say**)

9. Let me finish_____ this postcard to Aunt Mary. (**write**)

| | Verbs Followed by | |
Infinitives	Prepositions	
Verbs Followed by		Verbs Followed by an Object
Infinitives		and an Infinitive

10. Do you mind_____ here while I run into the store to buy some

    gum? (**stay**)

11. Last night we discussed_____ our jobs and traveling around the

    world. (**quit**)

12. You should consider_____ Siena while you're in Florence. (**visit**)

    ANSWER KEY

    1. being; 2. playing; 3. making; 4. singing; 5. going; 6. asking; 7. driving; 8. saying; 9. writing; 10. staying; 11. quitting; 12. visiting

✎ Drive It Home

Fill in the spaces below with the gerunds of the verbs provided.

1. He doesn't like me_____ late at night. (**drive**)

2. Me_____ to her is not going to make things better. (**talk**)

3. They are talking about_____ to Mallorca this autumn. (**go**)

4. We were proud of him for_____ smoking. (**quit**)

5. Are you going to ask him about_____ his parents? (**visit**)

6. _____ into the hotel was so easy. (**check**)

7. _____ to go to the store all the time is driving me nuts. (**have**)

8. You risk_____ your plane if you wait any longer. (**miss**)

9. Have you considered_____ to write? (**try**)

10. They enjoyed_____ the sights around town. (**see**)

    ANSWER KEY

    1. driving; 2. talking; 3. going; 4. quitting; 5. visiting; 6. Checking; 7. Having; 8. missing;

    9. trying; 10. seeing

How Did You Do?

Let's see how you did in this lesson. By now, you should be able to:

☐ form and use gerunds as nouns (Still unsure? Jump back to page 279.)

☐ use gerunds with verbs (Still unsure? Jump back to page 284.)

☐ use possessors to modify gerunds (Still unsure? Jump back to page 285.)

✎ Word Recall

Match the gerunds in the left column to their best match in the right column below.

1. standing	a. on vacation
2. complaining	b. to music
3. dreaming	c. of wonderful things
4. checking in	d. your legs
5. listening	e. around a field
6. being	f. about the drive
7. stretching	g. in the sun
8. lying	h. to the hotel

ANSWER KEY
1. e; 2. f; 3. c; 4. h; 5. b; 6. a; 7. d; 8. g

Lesson 19: Sentences

In this lesson you'll learn how to:

☐ use infinitives with adjectives

☐ use infinitives with **too** and **enough**

☐ use verbs followed by infinitives

☐ use verbs followed by either infinitives or gerunds

Sentence Builder 1

▷ 19A Sentence Builder 1 (CD 6, Track 25)

We'll be arriving at the hotel too late to do anything.	
We should get to bed early enough to wake up tomorrow.	
Five hours is too long to drive without stopping.	
I'll be happy to call someone to bring your bags up to your room.	
We're eager to get up to our room and get settled in.	
I'd be disappointed not to be given a tour.	
Is it ever too cold to swim outdoors here?	
You'd be surprised to see how cold it can get here.	
They're eager to offer you vouchers for the restaurant.	
It's probably best to stay away from the hot stove.	
Are you anxious to work out?	
Is the bed comfortable enough to sleep in?	

✎ Sentence Practice 1

Listen again to Sentence Builder 1 and fill in the missing words or phrases in the blanks below.

1. We'll be arriving at the hotel_____

   _____.

2. We should get to bed_____

   _____ tomorrow.

3. Five hours is_____ without stopping.

4. I'll be_____ someone to bring your bags up to your

   room.

5. We're_____ up to our room and get settled in.

6. I'd be disappointed_____ a tour.

7. Is it ever_____ outdoors here?

8. You'd be_____ how cold it can get here.

9. They're_____ you vouchers for the restaurant.

10. It's probably best_____ the hot stove.

11. Are you_____ to work out?

12. Is the bed_____ to sleep in?

ANSWER KEY
1. **too late to do anything**; 2. **early enough to wake up**; 3. **too long to drive**; 4. **happy to call**; 5. **eager to get**; 6. **not to be given**; 7. **too cold to swim**; 8. **surprised to see**; 9. **eager to offer**; 10. **to stay away from**; 11. **anxious**; 12. **comfortable enough**

Infinitives

Verbs Followed by
Prepositions

Verbs Followed by
Infinitives

Verbs Followed by an Object
and an Infinitive

Grammar Builder 1

▶ 19B Grammar Builder 1 (CD 6, Track 26)

INFINITIVES

In Lesson 6 you learned that the to form of a verb (its infinitive) can be used to express purpose, and in Lesson 9 of *Essential English* you learned about using the infinitive with want, have, and need.

The flight leaves in an hour! We really need <u>to get</u> to the airport!	
Can you go to the supermarket <u>to buy</u> some milk and eggs?	

There is also a set of adjectives that are followed by the infinitive form of the verb.

afraid I'm afraid to know what you were doing last night.	
disappointed He was disappointed to learn that his trip had been canceled.	
happy We're happy to have you stay with us while you're in town.	
likely They're likely to spend their whole vacation lying in the sun.	
proud I'm proud to say I've never had a speeding ticket.	
ready Are you ready to go?	

surprised She was surprised to learn that he was in town.	

Other adjectives followed by the infinitive include: amazed, anxious, ashamed, astonished, careful, certain, delighted, determined, eager, glad, hesitant, horrified, liable, lucky, pleased, relieved, reluctant, sad, shocked, sorry, upset, willing

The infinitive can also be used as a subject of the sentence with any adjectives.

To worry about things you can't control is silly.	
To drive slowly in fog is best.	

Note, however, that it is more common to place the adjective first with it is in spoken English.

It is silly to worry about things you can't control.	
It's best to drive slowly in fog.	

Just as with gerunds, infinitives can be negated with the word not. This word usually comes before the to.

I'd be happy not to have to go to work today.	
We were disappointed not to be able to go skiing in the Alps.	

Infinitives are also used following too and enough to express cause and effect. Too comes before the cause that creates a negative effect.

It was too hot. I couldn't go outside. It was too hot to go outside.	

Verbs Followed by
Prepositions

Verbs Followed by
Infinitives

Verbs Followed by an Object
and an Infinitive

There are too many people here. She can't find you. There are too many people here to find you.	

Enough follows an adjective or precedes a noun and can suggest either a positive or negative result.

Is your bed comfortable enough? Can you sleep in it? Is your bed comfortable enough to sleep in?	
There are enough blankets. We can sleep comfortably. There are enough blankets to sleep comfortably.	

Notice that it/them is dropped when the effect verb is an infinitive.

It's too high. They can't reach it. It's too high to reach.	
The beds are comfortable enough. They can sleep in them. The beds are comfortable enough to sleep in.	

You can also add for me/you/him/her etc. between the cause and effect to clarify who you are talking about.

It was too hot for me to go outside.	
There are too many people here for her to find you.	
Is your bed comfortable enough for you to sleep in?	

| Yes, there are enough blankets for us to sleep comfortably. | |

Without these pronouns for clarification, the statement is more general.

✎ Work Out 1

Combine the sentences in each question below into one sentence using an infinitive.

1. It was too dark. I couldn't see.

   _____

2. There were too many options. She couldn't choose.

   _____

3. The shelf is too high. They can't reach it.

   _____

   These pants are too tight. He can't wear them.

   _____

4. Are there enough bread rolls? Can we all eat?

   _____

5. It's light enough in here. I can read.

   _____

6. We have enough money. We can stay an extra night in the hotel.

   _____

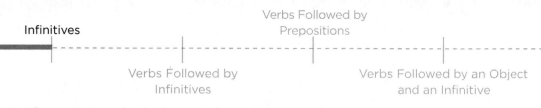

Infinitives

Verbs Followed by
Prepositions

Verbs Followed by
Infinitives

Verbs Followed by an Object
and an Infinitive

7. The music is too loud. They can't hear what I'm saying.

_____

8. This coffee is too sweet. I can't drink it.

_____

9. Is it cool enough in here? Are you comfortable?

_____

ANSWER KEY
1. It was too dark (for me) to see. 2. There were too many options (for her) to choose. 3. The shelf is too high (for them) to reach. 4. These pants are too tight (for him) to wear. 5. Are there enough bread rolls (for us all) to eat? 6. It's light enough in here (for me) to read. 7. We have enough money (for us) to stay an extra night in the hotel. 8. The music is too loud (for them) to hear what I'm saying. 9. This coffee is too sweet (for me) to drink. 10. Is it cool enough in here (for you) to be comfortable?

Sentence Builder 2

▶ 19C Sentence Builder 2 (CD 6, Track 27)

It all starts to look the same after a few miles.	
There's nothing I can do to make it more interesting.	
I promise to relax and enjoy the sun.	
Promise to pull off the highway for a break soon.	
Can I convince you to relax in your room?	
He asked me to call room service.	
They decided to go to a resort on their vacation.	
She refuses to come with us this year.	

Do you like staying in hotels, or do you like to stay at resorts when on vacation?	
We should try to reserve the hotel rooms early.	
Did you remember to ask our neighbors to water the plants?	
I don't remember locking the doors before we left.	

✎ Sentence Practice 2

Listen again to Sentence Builder 2 and fill in the missing words or phrases in the blanks below.

1. It all_____ the same after a few miles.

2. There's nothing I can do_____.

3. I_____ and enjoy the sun.

4. _____ the highway for a break soon.

5. Can I_____ in your room?

6. He_____room service.

7. They_____ to a resort on their vacation.

8. She_____ with us this year.

9. Do you like staying in hotels, or do you_____

_____ when on vacation?

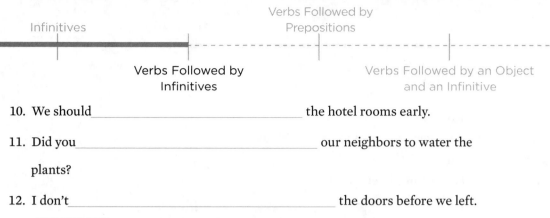

Infinitives

Verbs Followed by Prepositions

Verbs Followed by Infinitives

Verbs Followed by an Object and an Infinitive

10. We should_____ the hotel rooms early.

11. Did you_____ our neighbors to water the

plants?

12. I don't_____ the doors before we left.

ANSWER KEY

1. **starts to look**; 2. **to make it more interesting**; 3. **promise to relax**; 4. **Promise to pull off**; 5. **convince you to relax**; 6. **asked me to call**; 7. **decided to go**; 8. **refuses to come**; 9. **like to stay at resorts**; 10. **try to reserve**; 11. **remember to ask**; 12. **remember locking**

Grammar Builder 2

⊙ 19D Grammar Builder 2 (CD 6, Track 28)

VERBS FOLLOWED BY INFINITIVES

As you saw in Lesson 18, certain verbs are followed by gerunds. There is also a group of verbs that must be followed by infinitives. Let's look at some of the most common ones.

decide They decided to go to a resort on their vacation.	
deserve She deserves to win the science fair; she had the best project.	
hope I hope to see you again soon!	
learn We are learning to speak English.	
need Do you need to stop and take a rest?	

promise He never promised to come with us.	
want They want to help us plant our garden this spring.	

Other common verbs followed by infinitives are: afford, agree, appear, ask, claim, consent, demand, expect, fail, manage, offer, plan, prepare, pretend, refuse, seem, volunteer, wait, wish.

Some of these verbs often include a pronoun or noun between the verb and the infinitive.

Will you ask him to pass the salt?	
We need them to drive us to the airport.	
I had expected him to handle the bills.	
Should we invite her to come with us?	
Remind me to water the plants before we go away.	
Promise us to behave while you're at the party.	
Do you want them to drive us to the airport?	

Other common verbs that can take a pronoun or noun before the infinitive:
advise, allow, convince, encourage, force, permit, require, tell, warn, would like.

Infinitives

Verbs Followed by
Prepositions

Verbs Followed by
Infinitives

Verbs Followed by an Object
and an Infinitive

Take It Further
VERBS FOLLOWED BY GERUNDS OR INFINITIVES

There is also a group of verbs that can be followed by either an infinitive or a gerund.

begin **We'll begin studying for our test on Friday.** **We'll begin to study for our test on Friday.**	
like **I like eating peanut butter and jelly.** **I like to eat peanut butter and jelly.**	
prefer **Do you prefer driving during the day?** **Do you prefer to drive during the day?**	
start **They started taking the train into the city.** **They started to take the train into the city.**	

Some other common verbs that are followed by either an infinitive or a gerund are **continue, forget, hate, love, remember, can't stand, try.**

Note that the verbs forget, remember, try, and regret have different meanings depending on whether the verb is followed by a gerund or an infinitive.

forget/remember Did you forget/remember to take out the trash? (It is unknown whether the trash got taken out; did you forget/remember to do it?) Did you forget/remember taking out the trash? (The trash was taken out; did you forget/remember it happened?)	
regret We regret to inform you that your application has been denied. (We are informing you of bad news.) We regret informing you that your application was denied. (We regret that we told you.)	
try You should try to be nicer. (You should make an effort to be nicer.) You should try being nicer. (You should try a new approach by being nicer.)	

Infinitives

Verbs Followed by
Prepositions

Verbs Followed by
Infinitives

Verbs Followed by an Object
and an Infinitive

✎ Work Out 2

Fill in the blanks below with the verb in its correct form. If both a gerund and an infinitive are possible, enter both possible answers.

1. Remind me_____ the neighbors to water our plants. (ask)

2. Will you promise_____ me when I'm back home? (visit)

3. Do you need me_____ you to the airport? (drive)

4. They like_____ on vacation in July. (go)

5. He is going to ask her_____ for the test with him. (study)

6. I can't stand_____ in the rain. (walk)

7. Are you refusing_____ with us on this trip? (come)

8. She regrets not_____ that vacation last year. (take)

9. We failed_____ the hotel room in time for our trip.
   (reserve)

10. We prefer_____ in a resort when we go on
    vacation. (stay)

11. She asked them to continue_____ while she
    prepared the dessert. (eat)

12. These plants are dry. Did you remember_____ them? (water)

ANSWER KEY
1. to ask; 2. to visit; 3. to drive; 4. going/to go; 5. to study; 6. walking/to walk; 7. to come; 8. taking; 9. to reserve; 10. staying/to stay; 11. eating/to eat; 12. to water

✎ Drive It Home

Fill in the blanks below with the best form of the verb **drive** to complete each sentence.

1. We need_____ the kids to school today.

2. Remind me_____ slowly; I don't want to get a ticket.

3. I'm anxious_____ up the coast this weekend.

4. She said she was happy_____me to the airport.

5. It's too snowy_____.

6. We were reluctant_____ that far without stopping.

7. Promise_____ safely!

8. Do we have enough gas_____ to the store?

9. It's best not_____ during a heavy thunderstorm.

10. They decided_____ to Tampa on the weekend.

ANSWER KEY
all **to drive**

How Did You Do?

Let's see how you did in this lesson. By now, you should be able to:

☐ use infinitives with adjectives (Still unsure? Jump back to page 291.)

☐ use infinitives with **too** and **enough** (Still unsure? Jump back to page 292.)

Verbs Followed by Infinitives   Verbs Followed by an Object and an Infinitive

- ☐ use verbs followed by infinitives (Still unsure? Jump back to page 297.)

- ☐ use verbs followed by either infinitives or gerunds (Still unsure? Jump back to page 299.)

✎ Word Recall

Let's remind ourselves of some words related to car travel. Match the word in the left column with its best match in the right column.

1. exit ramp	a. freeway
2. highway	b. route
3. rush hour	c. disconnect
4. map	d. brake
5. unwind	e. entrance ramp
6. miles	f. swerve
7. gas pedal	g. yards
8. veer	h. traffic

ANSWER KEY
1. e; 2. a; 3. h; 4. b; 5. c; 6. g; 7. d; 8. f

Lesson 20: Conversations

By the end of this lesson, you should be able to:

- ☐ use verbs followed by specific prepositions

- ☐ use verbs followed by an object + and infinitive

- ☐ distinguish the verb pairs raise/rise, sit/set, lie/lay

Conversation 1

▶ 20A Conversation 1 (CD 6, Track 29)

Alison and Tom have started their vacation. They're in the car, driving to their beach getaway. Listen in.

Alison:	Ugh! We've been driving in the car for three hours. How much longer will we be driving?
Tom:	The GPS says we'll be there in about two hours. I think we can rely on that, unless we run into traffic.
Alison:	Two more hours? I'm tired of sitting here, just looking out the window.
Tom:	Well don't get annoyed at me!
Alison:	I'm not annoyed at you. I'm just not used to sitting for so long, and I'm bored with this drive.
Tom:	Oh, come on. I enjoy driving. I love seeing the sights and driving through areas that I'm not familiar with.
Alison:	What sights? It all starts to look the same after a few miles. Hey look! There's another sign. And another truck. And there's another exit ramp. And check that out! Another group of cows standing around in a field.
Tom:	Stop complaining about the scenery. There's nothing I can do to make it more interesting. Instead of looking out the window, you can take advantage of the time by reading, by listening to music, or by dreaming of all the wonderful things you'll be doing on vacation tonight.
Alison:	Tomorrow. We'll be arriving at the hotel too late to do anything tonight.
Tom:	Fine. Tonight we'll unpack, have a nice dinner, and get to bed early enough to wake up tomorrow and get right out on the beach. You'll be lying in the sun and I'll be swimming all day tomorrow.

Infinitives

Verbs Followed by
Prepositions

Verbs Followed by
Infinitives

Verbs Followed by an Object
and an Infinitive

Alison:	Well, I am excited about being on vacation. A whole week without work, without e-mails, without phone calls . . .
Tom:	Actually, I'll be calling in for a meeting or two.
Alison:	You'll be working this week? You're on vacation! Can't you disconnect from the office for a week?
Tom:	You know I'm not crazy about having to work over vacation, but I don't have a choice. And last winter, if I remember correctly, you had to call into the office once or twice when we were skiing.
Alison:	I suppose you have a point.
Tom:	It's just one or two phone calls. I promise to relax and enjoy the sun for the rest of the time.
Alison:	Okay, but promise to do one other thing.
Tom:	What's that?
Alison:	Promise to pull off the highway for a break soon. Five hours is too long to drive without stopping.
Tom:	Well, we'll need gas at some point soon, so keep an eye out for a rest stop.
Alison:	Perfect. I look forward to stretching my legs a bit. And maybe there will be some nice cows to look at.

✎ Conversation Practice 1

Answer the questions below based on Conversation 1.

1. How long have they been in the car?

_____

2. Why does Tom enjoy driving?

_____

3. What does Alison say she sees apart from a sign, a truck, and a group of cows standing in a field?

_____

4. How else does Tom suggest Alison take advantage of the time besides looking out the window?

_____

5. What will they do tonight?

_____

6. What will they be doing tomorrow?

_____

7. Will Tom spend his vacation not working?

_____

8. Where did they go on vacation last winter?

_____

9. How long does Alison think is too long to drive without stopping?

_____

10. What is Alison looking forward to when they stop?

_____

ANSWER KEY

1. They have been in the car for three hours. 2. He loves seeing the sights and driving through areas he's not familiar with. 3. She sees another exit ramp. 4. He says she can take advantage of the time by reading, listening to music, or dreaming of all the wonderful things she'll be doing on vacation. 5. They'll unpack, have a nice dinner, and get to bed early. 6. Alison will be lying in the sun, and Tom will be swimming all day. 7. No, he'll be calling in for a meeting or two. 8. They went skiing. 9. She thinks five hours is too long to drive without stopping. 10. She is looking forward to stretching her legs.

Verbs Followed by Infinitives

Verbs Followed by an Object and an Infinitive

⊕ Culture Note
THE AMERICAN ROAD TRIP

Ever since Henry Ford started rolling automobiles off his assembly line at the beginning of the twentieth century, Americans have been in love with their cars. In the 1950s, President Eisenhower unified the highways to create the interstate system, connecting the whole country by one system of nationally maintained roads. They say this led to the tradition of the American road trip. There are so many sites to see, and so many places to visit, some people take weeks or even months (if they can find the vacation time) to travel across the country in their cars. Many people travel shorter distances (5–7 hours) by car instead of taking a plane. Along the road, you can visit roadside attractions, national monuments and parks, diners, small towns, and scenic overlooks. The American landscape is so vast and varied; if you decide to take a road trip you will be seeing deserts, plains, and mountains, even within a day's drive. Just remember that it's important to take breaks when you drive long distances, so while you're visiting America's roadside attractions, be sure to visit its rest areas too!

Grammar Builder 1
▶ 20B Grammar Builder 1 (CD 6, Track 30)

VERBS FOLLOWED BY PREPOSITIONS

There are some verbs in English that are followed by certain prepositions. These are different from phrasal verbs, which you learned about in Lesson 14; the meaning of the verb doesn't change. Let's look at some of the more common ones.

rely on	
I hope we can rely on the neighbors to remember to water our plants.	

look forward to She's really looking forward to this vacation.	
plan on/for Do you plan on being away for a long time?	
apologize for They apologized for breaking the window.	
focus on If we focus on finishing the project, we can go home.	
believe in Do you believe in ghosts?	
care about/for If you care about safety, you should drive slowly.	
feel like I feel like eating Chinese food!	
forget about Don't forget about meeting me for dinner on Thursday.	
respond to Did we ever respond to their email?	

Some other common verb and preposition pairs are: agree with, apply to/ for, approve of, argue with/about, blame for, compare to, complain about, contribute to, cover with, decide (up)on, depend (up)on, dream of/about, escape from, excuse for, hope for, insist (up)on, object to, prevent from, protect from, stop from, subscribe to, take care of, thank for, vote for.

Verbs Followed by
Prepositions

Infinitives

Verbs Followed by
Infinitives

Verbs Followed by an Object
and an Infinitive

Some of these prepositional verbs are used with the direct object or direct object pronoun between the verb and the preposition.

bore with I don't want to bore you with the details.	
blame for She blamed him for forgetting the suitcase.	
compare to She wishes he wouldn't compare her to his last girlfriend.	
cover with He covered the wood with a tarp.	
excuse for You'll have to excuse us for not being more prepared.	
prevent from If you want to prevent the food from spoiling, put it in the refrigerator.	
protect from Wearing a helmet when you ride a bike will protect you from head injuries.	
put through Can you put me through to the concierge?	
stop from Stop me from eating all of this cake!	

thank for Be sure to thank Aunt Mary for the gift.	
talk into You've talked your father into seeing the new Scorsese movie.	

✎ Work Out 1

Choose the appropriate preposition to complete the sentence.

1. Do you agree_____ me?

    a. to

    b. of

    c. for

    d. with

2. All we can do is hope_____ the best.

    a. with

    b. for

    c. in

    d. to

3. He has been taking care_____ his daughter since she was two years old.

    a. for

    b. with

Infinitives		Verbs Followed by Prepositions	
	Verbs Followed by Infinitives		Verbs Followed by an Object and an Infinitive

c. of

d. in

4. They didn't have anyone to blame_____ the mistake.

  a. for

  b. about

  c. by

  d. of

5. Do you object_____ this paint color for the dining room?

  a. to

  b. of

  c. with

  d. for

6. I don't subscribe_____ any magazines.

  a. of

  b. with

  c. to

  d. in

7. Last night I dreamed_____ a beautiful beach.

  a. in

  b. for

  c. about

  d. to

8. They haven't decided_____where they will be staying on their vacation.

a. of

b. on

c. in

d. to

9. Each of us contributed_____ this project.

a. with

b. to

c. for

d. of

10. I don't approve_____ the amount of time you spend playing video games.

a. for

b. in

c. of

d. with

ANSWER KEY
1. d; 2. b; 3. c; 4. a; 5. a; 6. c; 7. c; 8. b; 9. b; 10. c

Conversation 2

▶ 20C Conversation 2 (CD 6, Track 31)

Alison and Tom have arrived at their seaside hotel, and they're ready to begin their vacation. Listen in.

Front Desk Clerk: Welcome to the Windward Resort, folks. How can I
help you?

Infinitives

Verbs Followed by
Prepositions

Verbs Followed by
Infinitives

Verbs Followed by an Object
and an Infinitive

Tom: Hi there. We're checking in. Tom and Alison Martinson.

Front Desk Clerk: Tom and Alison Martinson... Yes, here we go. I see that you'll be staying with us for six nights.

Alison: That's right, checking out on the morning of the fourteenth.

Front Desk Clerk: Okay. You can just set your bags right there, and I'll be happy to call someone to bring them up to your room, number 74, which is on the top floor. You won't be disappointed with the view from your balcony!

Tom: That's great. We're eager to get up to our room and get settled in.

Alison: And then have something to eat.

Front Desk Clerk: Absolutely. We'll take good care of you. But before you go up to your room, can I provide you with any information about the resort? Are you familiar with the amenities?

Tom: Well, no, we haven't been here before, so maybe you can show us around quickly.

Front Desk Clerk: I'd be happy to give you a quick tour. Just come with me. Right through those doors there is the Sunrise Room, which looks out over the beach. We serve breakfast in there from six thirty until nine, but I recommend getting there by seven or seven thirty if you want a table by the window. It fills up quickly.

Alison: I think I'll be too tired tomorrow morning for such an early breakfast, but we'll manage to wake up early enough later in the week.

Front Desk Clerk: You should consider doing that toward the middle of the week; there will be fewer people at the hotel then.

Tom: Oh, I see a great pool through those windows over there.

Front Desk Clerk: That's right. The hotel is actually equipped with two pools, one outdoor and one indoor.

Alison: Is it ever too cold to swim outdoors here?

Front Desk Clerk: Oh, you'd be surprised to see how cold it can get here in the winter. It never snows, but the water is certainly chilly. So, with a heated indoor pool, we provide our guests with the option of swimming all year long. Do you anticipate swimming much?

Tom: Absolutely! I plan on swimming every day. But I also like working out. Does the hotel have a gym or a workout room?

Front Desk Clerk: It does, but we're renovating it right now. I apologize for that. But we're happy to provide you with vouchers for a nearby gym. It's very modern and convenient, if you decide to take advantage of it.

Alison: Tom, you're on vacation! Are you anxious to work out?

Tom: Speaking of work, I assume the hotel has WiFi?

Front Desk Clerk: Absolutely. There's also a business center with several computers, a fax machine, a scanner, a conference room…

Alison: I think we're going to do our best to stay away from there.

Front Desk Clerk: Well, it's there if you need to use it, but we keep it hidden away so you can focus on enjoying your vacation. Now, you said that you were anxious to have some dinner. We have a wonderful restaurant that we're very proud of, but can I convince you to relax in your room and call for room service tonight?

Tom: You can convince me of doing that very easily!

Alison: I'm convinced already. I think room service on that balcony with the beautiful view sounds perfect.

Front Desk Clerk: Perfect. Here are your key cards, the elevators are right over there to the left, and just let me know if you think of anything that I can do for you.

Infinitives

Verbs Followed by
Prepositions

Verbs Followed by
Infinitives

Verbs Followed by an Object
and an Infinitive

✎ Conversation Practice 2

Answer the questions below based on Conversation 2.

1. For how many nights are Tom and Alison staying at the Windward Resort?

   _____

2. When will they be checking out?

   _____

3. What room number are they staying in, and on what floor is it?

   _____

4. What does the Sunrise Room look out over?

   _____

5. When is breakfast served?

   _____

6. How many pools are there?

   _____

7. Does Tom anticipate swimming much?

   _____

8. Why can't Tom use the gym or workout room at the hotel?

   _____

9. What can you find in the business center?

   _____

10. What does the front desk clerk convince Tom and Alison to do instead of going to

    the restaurant? _____

The Future Progressive
Gerunds

Adjectives Followed
by Prepositions

Verbs Followed by
Gerunds

ANSWER KEY
1. They are staying for six nights. 2. They will be checking out the morning of the fourteenth. 3. They are in room number 74, on the top floor. 4. The Sunrise Room looks out over the beach. 5. Breakfast is served from six-thirty until nine. 6. There are two pools, one indoor and one outdoor. 7. Yes, he plans on swimming every day. 8. He can't use it because they are renovating right now. 9. There are several computers, a fax machine, a scanner, and a conference room. 10. The front desk clerk convinces them to relax in their room and call for room service.

Grammar Builder 2
▶ 20D Grammar Builder 2 (CD 6, Track 32)

VERBS FOLLOWED BY AN OBJECT AND AN INFINITIVE

In Lesson 19, you saw verbs followed by infinitives. Some of these verbs can also be followed by an object before the infinitive. Let's look at some common examples.

advise They advised me to take a vacation.	
allow Their mother won't allow them to stay out later than eight o'clock.	
ask Did you ask them to drive you to the airport?	
bring Let's bring him to see the new exhibit at the museum.	
choose We chose the best singer to sing the lead on this song.	
expect They expected me to be there at eight.	

Verbs Followed by Infinitives	Verbs Followed by an Object and an Infinitive
remind **Remind me to feed the fish.**	
teach **The professor was teaching them to speak Arabic.**	
tell **Tell them to stop doing that.**	
urge **We urge you to take a break.**	
want **They want me to take care of their house while they're away.**	

Other verbs that take an object before the infinitive are: beg, challenge, command, dare, direct, encourage, forbid, force, hire, invite, order, persuade, prepare, require, send, warn.

Take It Further
CONFUSING VERB PAIRS

There are some verb pairs in English that can be confusing even to native speakers. Lay, set, and raise are all transitive verbs, meaning they are followed by an object, while lie, sit, and rise are intransitive, meaning they are not followed by an object. Let's look at the differences between them.

LAY/LIE

Lay means to place, while lie means to recline.

She lays the towel on the ground. (The towel is on the ground.)	
She lies on the ground. (She herself is on the ground.)	

This can be confusing in the past tense: the past of lie is lay.

She lay on the ground. (past)	

The past tense of lay is laid; its participle is also laid. The participle of lie is lain.

She laid the towel on the ground. The towel has been laid.	
She has lain on the ground.	

SET/SIT

Set means to place, and sit means to seat oneself.

I set the book on the chair.	
I sit on the chair.	

The past tense and participle of set are both set; the past tense and participle of sit are sat.

I set the book on the chair. I have set the book on the chair.	
I sat on the chair. I have sat on the chair.	

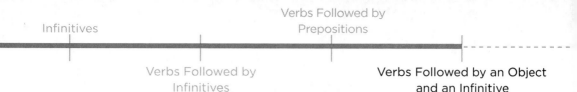
RAISE/RISE

Raise means to lift, and rise means to make oneself stand.

They raise the flag on the flagpole.	
The sun rises in the morning.	

The past tense and participle of raise are raised; the past tense of rise is rose and the participle is risen.

They raised the flag on the flagpole. The flag was raised.	
The sun rose in the morning. The sun has risen.	

✎ Work Out 2

Finish the sentences from the clues below.

Example: They drive us to the airport. We asked ...
Answer: **We asked them to drive us to the airport.**

1. They do their homework. We urged ...

   _____

2. He is on time. I told ...

   _____

3. They speak French. He taught ...

   _____

4. We visit our parents. She encourages . . .

5. The kids don't touch the stove. He warned . . .

6. She doesn't go out past eight. They forbade . . .

7. You listen to this song. I wanted . . .

8. I take out the trash. Remind . . .

9. The room is cleaned. He expects . . .

10. We are coming to the party. He invited . . .

ANSWER KEY

1. We urged them to do their homework. 2. I told him to be on time. 3. He taught them to speak French. 4. She encourages us to visit our parents. 5. He warned the kids not to touch the stove. 6. They forbade her to go out past eight. 7. I wanted you to listen to this song. 8. Remind me to take out the trash. 9. He expects the room to be cleaned. 10. He invited us to come to the party.

Infinitives

Verbs Followed by
Prepositions

Verbs Followed by
Infinitives

Verbs Followed by an Object
and an Infinitive

✎ Drive It Home

Lie or **lay**? Choose the best word to complete each of the sentences below.

1. Did you_____ the knives and forks on the table?

2. We_____ the blanket on the bed.

3. I will_____ a tablecloth on the picnic table.

4. You should_____ the book down while I'm talking.

5. We will_____ flowers on the grave.

6. I_____ on the bed.

7. We_____ in the sun.

8. They decided to_____ down and take a nap.

9. _____ here beside me and try to sleep.

10. If you want to get in the shade, you can_____ under that tree.

ANSWER KEY
1-5 all lay 6-10 all lie

How Did You Do?

Let's see how you did in this lesson. By now, you should be able to:

☐ use verbs followed by specific prepositions (Still unsure? Jump back to page 307.)

☐ use verbs followed by an object + and infinitive (Still unsure? Jump back to page 316.)

☐ distinguish the verb pairs raise/rise, sit/set, lie/lay (Still unsure? Jump back to page 317.)

✎ Word Recall

Let's remind ourselves of some vacation words. Match the word in the left column to its best match in the right column.

1. gym	a. workout room
2. bellhop	b. garden view
3. whirlpool	c. porter
4. indoor	d. single
5. ocean view	e. hot tub
6. double	f. outdoor

ANSWER KEY
1. a; 2. c; 3. e; 4. f; 5. b; 6. d

Don't forget to practice and reinforce what you've learned by visiting **www.livinglanguage.com/languagelab** for flashcards, games, and quizzes!

Unit 5 Quiz

Let's put the most essential English words and grammar points you've learned so far to practice in a few exercises. It's important to be sure that you've mastered this material before you move on. Score yourself at the end of the review and see if you need to go back for more practice, or if you're ready to move on to *Advanced English*.

A. Choose the correct tense of the verb in parentheses to complete each sentence.

1. We_____ for you when you get there. (wait)

2. They_____ Jim while they're in town. (see)

3. When I graduate from college, you_____ high school. (start)

B. Fill in the blank with the missing preposition.

1. Are you interested_____ seeing that exhibition?

2. You need to focus_____ driving.

3. I feel_____ going skiing this winter.

4. He was known_____ his sharp wit.

5. Don't forget_____ our trip to California next week.

6. They were very pleased_____ the hotel.

7. Do you agree_____ me?

C. For each sentence below, fill in the missing gerund, infinitive, or both where possible.

1. We've started_____ more. (exercise)

2. If you keep_____ that, I'll stop the car. (do)

3. I want her_____ with me to the movies tonight. (go)

4. He was too tired_____. (work)

5. Do you like_____ long distances? (drive)

6. She hopes_____ a new language this year. (learn)

7. Let's finish_____ dinner. (eat)

8. Is this bed comfortable enough_____ in? (sleep)

9. Tell them_____ a break while they're driving such a long distance. (take)

10. Do you remember_____ this bed? I can't remember where we got it. (buy)

ANSWER KEY
A. 1. will be waiting/are going to be waiting; 2. will be seeing/are going to be seeing; 3. will be starting/are going to be starting
B. 1. in; 2. on; 3. like; 4. for; 5. about; 6. with; 7. with
C. 1. exercising/to exercise; 2. doing; 3. to go; 4. to work; 5. driving/to drive; 6. to learn; 7. eating; 8. to sleep; 9. to take; 10. buying

How Did You Do?

Give yourself a point for every correct answer, then use the following key to tell whether you're ready to move on:

0–7 points: It's probably a good idea to go back through the lesson again. You may be moving too quickly, or there may be too much "down time" between your contact with English. Remember that it's better to spend 30 minutes with English three or four times a week than it is to spend two or three hours just once a week. Find a pace that's comfortable for you, and spread your contact hours out as much as you can.

8–12 points: You would benefit from a review before moving on. Go back and spend a little more time on the specific points that gave you trouble. Re-read the Grammar Builder sections that were difficult, and do the work out one more time. Don't forget about the online supplemental practice material, either. Go to **www.livinglanguage.com/languagelab** for games and quizzes that will reinforce the material from this unit.

13–17 points: Good job! There are just a few points that you could consider reviewing before moving on. If you haven't worked with the games and quizzes on **www.livinglanguage.com/languagelab**, please give them a try.

18–20 points: Great! You're ready to move on to Advanced English.

 points

Grammar Summary

1. IRREGULAR VERBS

Each of the following verbs appear in the infinitive, the simple past, and the past participial forms.

arise/arose/arisen	
awake/awoke/awoke	
be (am, are, is)/was, were/been	
beat/beat/beaten	
become/became/become	
begin/began/begun	
bend/bent/bent	
bet/bet/bet	
bid/bid/bid	
bind/bound/bound	
bite/bit/bitten	
bleed/bled/bled	
blow/blew/blown	
break/broke/broken	
bring/brought/brought	
build/built/built	
burst/burst/burst	
buy/bought/bought	
cast/cast/cast	
catch/caught/caught	
choose/chose/chosen	
cling/clung/clung	

Advanced English

come/came/come	
cost/cost/cost	
creep/crept/crept	
cut/cut/cut	
deal/dealt/dealt	
dig/dug/dug	
do/did/done	
draw/drew/drawn	
eat/ate/eaten	
fall/fell/fallen	
feed/fed/fed	
feel/felt/felt	
fight/find/fought	
find/found/found	
fit/fit/fit	
flee/fled/fled	
fling/flung/flung	
fly/flew/flown	
forbid/*forbade/forbidden	
forget/forgot/forgotten	
forgive/forgave/forgiven	
freeze/froze/frozen	
get/got/**gotten	
give/gave/given	
go/went/gone	
grind/ground/ground	
grow/grew/grown	
hang/hung/hung	

have/had/had	
hear/heard/heard	
hide/hid/hidden	
hit/hit/hit	
hold/held/held	
hurt/hurt/hurt	
keep/kept/kept	
kneel/knelt, kneeled/knelt, kneeled	
know/knew/known	
lay/laid/laid	
lead/led/led	
lean/leaned, leant/leaned, leant	
leave/left/left	
lend/lent/lent	
let/let/let	
light/lit, lighted/lit, lighted	
lose/lost/lost	
make/made/made	
mean/meant/meant	
meet/met/met	
misspell/misspelled/misspelled	
mistake/mistook/mistaken	
misunderstand/misunderstood/ misunderstood	
overthrow/overthrew/overthrown	
pay/paid/paid	
prove/proved/proven, proved	
put/put/put	

quit/quit, quitted/quit, quitted	
read/read/read	
rid/rid/rid	
ride/rode/ridden	
ring/rang/rung	
rise/rose/risen	
run/ran/run	
say/said/said	
see/saw/seen	
seek/sought/sought	
sell/sold/sold	
send/sent/sent	
set/set/set	
shake/shook/shaken	
shine/shone/shone	
shoot/shot/shot	
show/showed/shown	
shrink/shrank/shrunk	
shut/shut/shut	
sing/sang/sung	
sit/sat/sat	
sleep/slept/slept	
slide/slid/slid	
speak/spoke/spoken	
speed/sped, speeded/sped, speeded	
spend/spent/spent	
spin/spun/spun	
spread/spread/spread	

spring/sprang/sprung	
stand/stood/stood	
steal/stole/stolen	
stick/stuck/stuck	
sting/stung/stung	
stink/stank/stunk	
strike/struck/stricken	
swear/swore/sworn	
sweep/swept/swept	
swim/swam/swum	
swing/swung/swung	
take/took/taken	
teach/taught/taught	
tear/tore/torn	
tell/told/told	
think/thought/thought	
tread/trod/trod, trodden	
throw/threw/thrown	
understand/understood/understood	
undertake/undertook/undertaken	
upset/upset/upset	
wake/woke/woken	
wear/wore/worn	
weave/wove/woven	
weep/wept/wept	
win/won/won	
wind/wound/wound	
withdraw/withdrew/withdrawn	

wring/wrung/wrung	
write/wrote/written	

*Some speakers often use forbid for simple past.

**Some speakers often say have got to meaning must, and in British English the form gotten does not exist.

2. ADJECTIVES FOLLOWED BY PREPOSITIONS

absent from	
accustomed to	
acquainted with	
addicted to	
afraid of	
angry at/with	
annoyed with	
ashamed of	
associated with	
aware of	
awful at	
blessed with	
bored with	
capable of	
cluttered with	
comfortable with	
committed to	
composed of	
concerned about	
committed to	
composed of	

concerned about	
connected to	
content with	
convinced of	
coordinated with	
crazy about	
crowded with	
curious about	
dedicated to	
devoted to	
different from	
disappointed in/with	
discriminated against	
divorced from	
done with	
dressed in	
engaged to	
enthusiastic about	
envious of	
equipped with	
excited about/by	
exposed to	
faithful to	
familiar with	
filled with	
finished with	
fond of	
frightened by	

Advanced English

friendly to/with	
furious about	
furnished with	
glad about	
good at	
grateful to/for	
guilty of	
hidden from	
innocent of	
interested in	
involved in	
jealous of	
known for	
limited in/to	
located in	
made of	
married to	
nervous about	
opposed to	
patient with	
pleased with	
polite to	
prepared for	
provided with	
proud of	
ready for	
related to	
relevant to	

remembered for	
responsible for	
safe from	
satisfied with	
scared of	
shocked by/at	
sorry for/about	
terrified of	
tired of	
unhappy about	
upset with	
used to	
worried about	

3. VERBS FOLLOWED BY PREPOSITIONS

accuse of	
admit to	
advise against	
agree with	
apologize for	
apply to/for	
approve of	
argue with/about	
arrive in/at	
ask for	
beg for	
believe in	

blame for	
care about/for	
choose between/among	
compare to/with	
complain about	
consist of	
contribute to	
count on/upon	
cover with	
deal with	
decide on	
depend on/upon	
die from	
distinguish from	
dream of/about	
drink to	
escape from	
excel in/at	
excuse for	
fall in love with	
feel like	
fight for	
forget about	
forgive for	
hide from	
hope for	
insist on/upon	
introduce to	

keep from	
know about	
listen to	
look after	
look forward to	
made from	
object to	
participate in	
pay attention to	
plan on	
pray for	
prevent from	
prohibit from	
protect from	
provide with	
recover from	
rely on/upon	
remind of	
rescue from	
resort to	
respond to	
search for	
shoot at	
stare at	
stop from	
subscribe to	
substitute for	
succeed in	

Advanced English

talk about	
take advantage of	
take care of	
thank for	
think of	
vote for	
wait for	
warn against	
wonder about	

4. VERBS FOLLOWED BY GERUNDS

admit	
advise	
appreciate	
avoid	
can't help	
consider	
continue	
delay	
deny	
detest	
discuss	
dislike	
enjoy	
escape	
explain	
feel like	

finish	
forgive	
give up	
hate	
imagine	
keep	
loathe	
mention	
mind	
miss	
postpone	
prevent	
prohibit	
propose	
quit	
recommend	
regret	
resent	
risk	
suggest	
support	
tolerate	
understand	

5. VERBS FOLLOWED BY AN INFINITIVE

afford	
agree	

appear	
arrange	
ask	
attempt	
can't wait	
choose	
dare	
decide	
deserve	
expect	
fail	
forget	
grow	
help	
hesitate	
hope	
hurry	
intend	
learn (how)	
manage	
mean	
need	
neglect	
offer	
pay	
plan	
pretend	
refuse	

request	
seem	
struggle	
swear	
tend	
threaten	
try	
volunteer	
wait	
want	
wish	
would like	

6. VERBS FOLLOWED BY AN OBJECT AND INFINITIVE

advise	
allow	
ask*	
cause	
challenge	
convince	
encourage	
expect*	
forbid	
force	
get	
help*	
invite	

order	
permit	
persuade	
require	
remind	
teach	
tell	
urge	
warn	
want*	

*can also be followed by an infinitive without an object

7. ADJECTIVES FOLLOWED BY AN INFINITIVE

afraid	
amazed	
angry	
ashamed	
delighted	
depressed	
disappointed	
disturbed	
eager	
excited	
glad	
happy	
lucky	
pleased	

proud	
ready	
reluctant	
sad	
shocked	
sorry	
upset	
unhappy	

8. VERBS FOLLOWED BY A GERUND OR AN INFINITIVE

begin	
can't stand	
continue	
forget*	
hate	
like	
love	
prefer	
remember*	
start	
stop*	
try (*)	

*these verbs can be followed by either gerund or infinitive but the meaning will change